MW01461562

Soup
for
All Seasons

108 Vegetarian Recipes

**Members of the
Institute of the Himalayan Tradition**

Yes International Publishers
Saint Paul, Minnesota

All rights reserved.
Copyright © 2009 by Yes International Publishers.

No part of this book may be reproduced or transmitted
in any form or by any means, electronic or mechanical,
including photocopying, recording, or any
information storage and retrieval system,
without written permission from the publisher
except in the case of brief quotations
embodied in critical articles and reviews.

For information and permissions address:

Yes International Publishers
1317 Summit Avenue
Saint Paul, MN 55105-2602
www.yespublishers.com
651-645-6808

Artwork by Lorraine Wells
Introduction by David Heitzman

ISBN: 978-0-936663-49-4

Printed in the United States of America

Introduction

The soup recipes in this little cookbook come from members of the
Institute of the Himalayan Tradition.
Here is how that happened:

The institute holds a *satsang* (gathering of people interested
in making progress on all levels) every Thursday evening.
Immediately afterwards during the colder, darker part of the year
(which in Minnesota is a significant period of time!),
hot soup and crackers are served to those who wish to stay
for this simple meal and the informal conversations which occur.

The soup is prepared and donated by the members,
who take turns each week according to a schedule
created by a particular stalwart member.
Rather often the diners comment upon the excellent quality of the soup
and express interest in obtaining the recipe.
Thus, over time members gradually recorded their recipes
and gave them to Ma Devi, one of the institute's spiritual teachers.
She typed them up on her trusty computer, while
Lorraine Wells generously provided the fantastic artwork.
Voila! This book.

The actual cooks might notice that the printed recipes
differ in some small respect from their original submissions.
It is true that a few changes were made.
The changes were, however, merely an inevitable part
of attempting to achieve some level of uniformity
throughout the whole cookbook.
As with any cookbook, feel free to make your own modifications
and write in the margins!

A hearty "thank you" to everyone who contributed
in any way
to this cookbook of 108 superb soups.

Universal Prayer before Meals

Om Brahmar panam Brahma havih
Brahmagnau Brahmana hutam
Brahmaivatena gantavyam
Brahma karma samadhina
Om shantih shantih shantih

The offering is to God.
God is the offering.
The offering is made into the fire which is God.
The offering is made by God.
God alone is the One to whom the offering is made.
When seen through samadhi, all this action is of God.
Om peace, peace, peace.

O God, bless this food so that it brings vitality
and energy to fulfill thy mission and serve humanity.
O God, bless this food so that we remain aware of Thee
within and without.
O God, bless this food so that we love all
and exclude none.
Bless those who have provided this food,
those who have prepared this food,
and those who will eat this food.
Bless all, my Lord.
Peace, peace, peace.

Fall Soups:

Creamy Butternut Soup	1
Butternut and Apple Bisque	2
Butternut Coconut Soup	3
Butternut Cider Soup	4
African Peanut Soup	5
Vegetable Bean Soup	6
Gypsy Soup	7
Moroccan Harira	8
Potato Carrot Soup	9
Potato Tomato Stew	10
Green Soup	11
Chili with Quinoa	12
Cream of Sweet Potato Soup	13
Turnip Soup	14
Cheesy Cauliflower Soup	15
Pumpkin Soup	16
Pumpkin Pecan Soup	17
Pumpkin Yogurt Soup	18
Pumpkin Harvest Soup	19
Carrot Soup	20
Gingered Carrot Soup	21
Black Bean Potato Soup	22
Black Bean Tomato Soup	23
Black Bean and Sweet Potato Chili	24
Lentil Rice Stew	25
Lentil Spinach Stew	26
Italian Lentil Soup	27
Miso Soup	28
Miso Noodle Soup	29
Adzuki Bean Miso Soup	30
Tofu Mixed Bean Soup	31
Tofu Chili	32
Navy Bean Chili	33
Navy Bean Vegetable Soup	34
White Bean Soup	35
Hearty Vegetable Stew	36

Winter Soups:

Acorn Squash Soup	37
Hubbard Squash Soup	38
Everything Soup	39
Candlemas Soup	40
Chunky Butternut Squash Soup	41
Harvest Carrot Soup	42
Creamy Leek Soup	43
Broccoli Potato Soup	44
Potato and Cider Soup	45
Potato Kale Soup	46
Potato Carrot Soup	47
Potato Cauliflower Soup	48
Potato Cheese Soup	49
Sweet Potato Kale Soup	50
Immune Booster Soup	51
Nepali Lentil Soup	52
Turkish Soup	53
Tofu and Barley Sherpa Soup	54
Mexistrone Soup	55
Pea Stew with Barley	56
Three Bean Treat	57
Orange Soup with No Oranges	58
Green Pea Soup	59
Split Pea Soup	60
Pinto Bean Stew	61
In-a-Hurry Black Bean Soup	62
Pasta Bean Soup	63
Roasted Root Soup	64
Vegetarian Chili	65
Vegetable Quinoa Soup	66
Wild Rice Soup	67
Wild Rice Squash Soup	68
Wild Rice Vegetable Soup	69
Vegetable Chowder	70
Sweet Onion Soup	71
Winter Squash Soup	72

Spring Soups:

Mixed Mushroom Soup 73
Mushroom Soup with Herbs 74
Cauliflower Soup 75
Tomato and Lime Soup 76
Feta Soup 77
Curried Chickpea Soup 78
Chili with Quinoa 79
Cream of Broccoli Soup 80
Creamy Spinach Soup 81
Corn Chowder 82
Corn Chowder with Vegetables 83
Greek Soup 84
Brown Rice and Broccoli Soup 85
Spinach Polenta Soup 86
Spinach and Lentil Soup 87
Spinach Soup with Basil and Dill 88
Vegetable Soup 89
Vegetable Bean Soup 90

Summer Soups:

Summer Soup 91
Fruit Soup 92
Avocado Soup 93
Chilled Avocado Soup 94
Cucumber Summer Soup 95
Cucumber Soup with Radish Confetti 96
Chilly Cucumber Soup 97
Chilled Cantaloupe Soup 98
Chilly Strawberry Soup 99
Chilled Radish Buttermilk Soup 100
Mint Pea Soup 101
Simple Spinach Soup 102
Gazpacho 103
Celery Apple Gazpacho 104
White Gazpacho 105
Zucchini Cucumber Soup 106
Curried Zucchini Soup 107
Cold Indian Lentil Soup 108

Index

Index 109

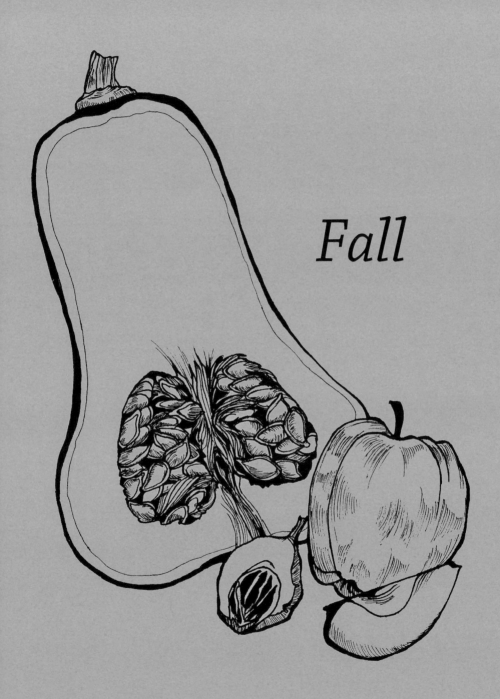

Fall

Creamy Butternut Soup

8 cups water
1 small butternut squash, peeled and cut into 1-inch cubes
½ cup rolled oats
1 Tbs. dried cilantro
1 Tbs. cumin powder
1 tsp. coriander powder
½ tsp. turmeric powder
½ tsp. black pepper
1 Tbs. grated fresh ginger
Juice of 1 lemon
1 Tbs. rock salt
1 Tbs. soy oil
2 scallions, chopped
Fresh parsley and watercress for garnish

Bring the water to a boil in a large heavy-bottomed pot.

Add squash, oats, cilantro, cumin, coriander, turmeric, black pepper, ginger, lemon, and salt. Cover and simmer on medium heat for 35 minutes.

Purée the squash.

Heat oil in a small skillet and sauté the scallions for about 2 minutes. Add them to the creamed soup. Cover and simmer five minutes more.

Serve hot garnished with fresh parsley and watercress.

Serves 6.

Butternut and Apple Bisque

3 Tbs. vegetable oil
2 Tbs. shallots, chopped
1 stalk celery, chopped
1 Granny Smith apple, peeled, cored, chopped
½ tsp. grated nutmeg
½ tsp. ground cinnamon
4 cups vegetable broth
3 cups butternut squash, peeled and diced
¼ cup cream (half and half works)

Soup Garnish:
1 tsp. butter
¼ tsp. grated nutmeg
¼ tsp. ground cinnamon
1 large Granny Smith apple, cored and diced

In a medium saucepan, heat oil. Cook shallots, celery, and apple until soft, about 5 minutes on medium heat. Stir in nutmeg and cinnamon and cook until fragrant, about 1 minute. Add squash and broth, bring to a boil, and then simmer about 30 minutes or until the squash is very tender.

Let the soup cool a bit, about 5 minutes, and then pour it into a blender or food processor. Add the cream and purée.

In a skillet, heat butter with nutmeg and cinnamon. Stir in the apple and sauté.

Garnish each bowl with the apple mixture when serving.

Serves 6.

Butternut Coconut Soup

1 large butternut squash, about 3 lbs.
1 Tbs. olive oil, plus 2 tsp. for coating the squash
1 large onion, diced
2½ Tbs. fresh ginger, grated
1 Tbs. ground coriander
1 tsp. ground cumin
½ tsp. turmeric
½ tsp. cinnamon
6 cups vegetable broth
1 tsp. salt
Ground black pepper
Juice of 1 lime
¼ cup chopped fresh basil
¼ cup chopped fresh cilantro
1 cup coconut milk

Preheat oven to 375 degrees F. Cut the squash in half and scoop out the seed. Brush the cut sides with olive oil and place cut-side-down on an oiled baking sheet. Bake until soft, about 40 minutes. Cool a bit and then scoop out the squash.

Heat the remaining olive oil in a soup pot over medium heat. Add the diced onion and grated ginger and stir while cooking until they are soft (about 8 minutes). Add coriander, cumin, turmeric, and cinnamon. Cook for another 2 minutes, continuing to stir.

Add squash, vegetable broth, salt, and pepper. Bring to a boil, then reduce heat to a simmer. Cook for another 10–15 minutes. Add lime juice, herbs, and coconut milk. Blend, adding more water if needed to reach desired consistency.

Taste and adjust seasoning to balance the salty, pungent, and citrus flavors. Ladle into bowls and garnish with extra coconut milk and coriander. Serves 4–5.

Butternut Cider Soup

5 Tbs. butter
2½ pounds butternut squash, peeled, seeded, cut into ½-inch
    pieces (about 6 cups)
2 cups chopped leeks
½ cup chopped carrots
½ cup chopped celery
2 Granny Smith apples, peeled, cored, chopped
1½ tsp. dried thyme
½ tsp. crumbled dried sage
5 cups vegetable broth
1½ cups apple cider
⅔ cup sour cream
½ cup whipping cream
Fresh chives, chopped

Melt butter in heavy saucepan over medium heat. Add squash, leeks, carrots, and celery. Sauté until slightly softened, about 15 minutes. Mix in apples, thyme, and sage. Add broth and 1 cup of cider. Bring to a boil. Reduce heat to medium-low. Cover and simmer until apples are tender, stirring occasionally, about 30 minutes. Cool slightly. Working in batches, purée soup in blender and return to pan.

Cider Cream: Boil remaining ½ cup cider in a heavy small saucepan until reduced to ¼ cup, about 5 minutes. Cool. Place sour cream in small bowl and whisk in cooled cider. (Cider cream can be made 1 day ahead; just cover separately and refrigerate.)

Bring soup to simmer. Mix in whipping cream. Ladle soup into bowls and drizzle with cider cream. Top with chives.

Serves 8–10.

African Peanut Soup

2 cups chopped onions
1 Tbs. peanut oil
½ tsp. cayenne or other ground dried chilies
1 tsp. grated peeled fresh ginger
1 cup chopped carrots
2 cups chopped sweet potatoes
4 cups vegetable broth
2 cups tomato juice
1 cup smooth peanut butter
1 Tbs. sugar (optional)
1½ cups chopped scallions or chives

Sauté onions in the oil until just translucent. Stir in cayenne and fresh ginger. Add carrots and sauté a few more minutes. Mix in sweet potatoes and broth, bring the soup to a boil, and then simmer for about 15 minutes, or until the vegetables are tender. Cool.

In a blender or food processor, purée the vegetables in batches with the cooking liquid and the tomato juice. Return the purée to a soup pot. Stir in the peanut butter until smooth. Taste the soup. Its sweetness will depend upon the sweetness of the carrots and sweet potatoes. If it's not there naturally, add just a little sugar to enhance the other flavors.

Reheat the soup gently, being careful not to scorch. Add more water or tomato juice for thinner soup.

Serve topped with plenty of chopped scallions or chives.

Serves 6.

Vegetable Bean Soup

3 cups water
1 28-oz. can whole Italian style tomatoes
2 medium leeks, sliced
1 Tbs. olive oil
8 oz. fresh mushrooms, quartered
1 large yellow or red pepper, coarsely chopped
4 garlic cloves, minced
1 15-oz. can white kidney beans (Cannellini), rinsed and drained
1 tsp. salt
¼ tsp. freshly ground black pepper
4 cups spinach leaves (about 8 oz.)

Coarsely chop the tomatoes, reserving the liquid from the can. In a 4-quart pot cook leeks in oil until tender, stirring occasionally. Add mushrooms, pepper, and garlic. Cook five minutes more. Add water, tomatoes, canning liquid, white beans, salt, and pepper. Stir and then bring to a boil.

Now simmer the soup, uncovered, for about 5 more minutes. Carefully stir in the spinach and serve.

Serves 6.

Gypsy Soup

3–4 Tbs. olive oil
2 cups chopped onion
2 cloves crushed garlic
2 cups chopped, peeled sweet potatoes
½ cup chopped celery
2 tsp. paprika
1 tsp. turmeric
1 tsp. basil
1 tsp. salt
dash of cinnamon
dash of cayenne pepper
1 bay leaf
3 cups vegetable broth or water
1 Tbs. tamari
1 cup chopped, fresh tomatoes
¾ cup chopped green peppers
1½ cups cooked chickpeas

In a soup kettle or large saucepan sauté onions, garlic, sweet potatoes and celery in olive oil for about 5 minutes.

Add the rest of the ingredients.

Simmer another 10 minutes or so until all the vegetables are as tender as you wish. Any orange vegetable can be combined with green. For example, peas or green beans could replace the peppers; carrots can be used instead of, or in addition to, the sweet potatoes.

Serves 4.

Moroccan Harira

2 Tbs. extra-virgin olive oil
1 medium onion, finely chopped
½ cup dried chickpeas, soaked in water overnight
8 cups homemade vegetable broth plus 4 cups water
3 garlic cloves, minced
2 Tbs. finely chopped and 1 Tbs. coarsely chopped fresh cilantro
3 tsp. coarse salt and ¼ tsp. freshly ground pepper
4 celery stalks, finely chopped
4 ripe tomatoes, peeled and chopped
1 cup yellow lentils
1 Tbs. tomato paste
1 Tbs. fresh lemon juice
1 cinnamon stick
½ tsp. sweet paprika
½ tsp. turmeric
½ tsp. ground ginger
½ tsp. coriander
⅛ tsp. ground cloves
5 oz. orzo or vermicelli noodles, broken into pieces
½ cup pitted dates, chopped
2 Tbs. coarsely chopped fresh parsley

Heat oil in a Dutch oven over medium heat. Add onion and cook 5 minutes. Add chickpeas, broth, and water, and simmer until tender, about 45 minutes.

Mash garlic, finely chopped cilantro, and salt into a paste. Add this paste, celery, tomatoes, lentils, tomato paste, lemon juice, and spices to pot. Simmer until the lentils are tender, 30 to 40 minutes.

Add pasta and dates, and cook until pasta is al dente, about 10 minutes. Stir in coarsely chopped cilantro and parsley. Garnish-

Potato Carrot Soup

2 medium garlic bulbs (about 16 cloves)
8 cups of broth
4 medium to large potatoes, peeled and cut into ½-inch cubes
4–5 carrots, scrubbed and sliced
½ cup soymilk
1 tsp. dried thyme
Freshly ground pepper to taste
Grated Cheddar cheese for topping (optional)

Separate garlic bulbs into cloves and peel them. In a large soup pot, combine broth, garlic, potatoes, carrots, and thyme. Bring to a boil; reduce heat. Simmer, covered, for 20–25 minutes or until vegetables are tender. Cool 5 minutes.

In a blender, purée about half of the soup until smooth. (Try to purée all of the large garlic cloves.) Return puréed soup to soup pot. Stir in soymilk.

Season to taste with freshly ground pepper.

Top with grated cheese, if desired.

Serves 6–8.

Potato Tomato Stew

1½ Tbs. olive oil
8 small red-skinned potatoes, quartered
1½ onions, finely chopped
2 large garlic cloves, finely chopped
¾ cup small brown or red lentils
2 cups diced tomatoes, including liquid
1 bay leaf
1 tsp. dried oregano
Salt and freshly ground pepper
½ cup basil leaves, loosely packed

Heat oil in a medium Dutch oven over medium-high heat. Add potatoes and cook until browned, about 10 minutes. Using tongs, remove the potatoes to a plate and set aside. Add onions to the pot, sauté for 5 minutes, and mix in garlic. Cook until the onions are browned, about 8 minutes, stirring often.

Add lentils, tomatoes with liquid, bay leaf, and oregano. Add 3 cups of cold water. Bring to a boil, reduce the heat, and simmer, uncovered, for 30 minutes.

Now add potatoes, and simmer until the potatoes and lentils are soft, about 30 minutes, adding ½ cup more water if needed. Remove the bay leaf, and season the stew to taste with salt and pepper.

To serve, sprinkle each bowl of soup with fresh basil.

Serves 4.

Green Soup

2 cups green split peas
1 parsnip, peeled and diced
1 yam or rutabaga, peeled and diced
2 small yellow onions, chopped
2 large baking potatoes, scrubbed and diced
1–2 turnips, peeled and diced
1 bunch broccoli
1 bunch fresh cilantro
1 bunch fresh parsley
3–4 carrots, scrubbed and diced
1 Tbs. dried basil
1 Tbs. coriander
2½ tsp. ground cumin
Salt and pepper to taste

Clean the split peas. Put them in a pot along with 4 quarts of water, parsnip, yam or rutabaga, onions, potatoes, and the turnips. Bring to a boil and cook for about 1 hour.

Next add broccoli, cilantro, parsley, and carrots, and cook for another 20 minutes.

Add the spices. Purée part or all of the soup, and serve hot.

Serves 12–14.

Chili with Quinoa

1 cup quinoa, well rinsed (about 3 times)
6 cups water
1 Tbs. canola or olive oil
1 large onion, chopped
1 medium green pepper, diced
1 cup celery, diced
2–3 large carrots, scrubbed and diced
2 tomatoes, diced (optional)
2 15-oz. cans kidney, adzuki, or black beans, drained
1 28-oz. can crushed tomatoes
1–2 Tbs. chili powder
1 Tbs. dried parsley
1 Tbs. dried oregano
2 tsp. ground cumin
¼ tsp. black pepper
½ tsp. salt

In a medium pan, combine quinoa and 2 cups of the water; cover the pan. Bring to a simmer, and cook for 15–20 minutes until all of the liquid is absorbed. Remove from heat, and let stand for about 10 minutes.

In a large pan, heat the oil and add onion, pepper, celery, and carrot. Cook for 7 minutes, stirring frequently.

Stir in 4 cups of water and the tomatoes, and cook for another 5 minutes. Stir in the beans, crushed tomatoes, and seasonings, and cook for about 25 minutes, over low heat, stirring occasionally.

Stir in the cooked quinoa, and heat for another 5 minutes.

Serves 6.

Cream of Sweet Potato Soup

2 Tbs. butter
3 green onions, thinly sliced
1 Tbs. all-purpose flour
2 cups broth
2½ cups cooked, puréed sweet potatoes (about 2 medium sized)
2 cups half and half
1 tsp. salt
⅛ tsp. yellow curry powder

Garnishes: chopped peanuts, sliced green onion

In heavy saucepan over medium heat, melt butter. Add green onions, and cook 2 minutes. Stir in flour, and cook 2 minutes, while stirring constantly. Stir in the broth and cook 5 minutes, stirring occasionally. Stir in sweet potatoes.

Process sweet potato mixture, in batches, in blender or food processor until smooth, stopping to scrape down the sides. Return mixture to the saucepan. Add half and half, salt, and yellow curry powder; and cook over low heat until thoroughly heated.

Garnish with peanuts and onion.

Serves 2–4.

Turnip Soup

1½ pounds small turnips
Salt
5 Tbs. butter
2–3 leeks, white parts only, sliced
6 branches thyme or ¼ tsp. dried thyme
4 cups milk
White or black pepper
2–3 cups turnip greens
Fresh chopped thyme for garnish

Peel the turnips and slice them into rounds about ¼ inch thick. Bring 3 quarts of water to a boil, and add 2 tsp. of salt together with the turnips. Cover and cook for 1 minute; drain.

Melt 3 Tbs. butter in a soup pot with ½ cup water. Add the leeks, turnips, thyme, and 1 tsp. salt. Cover and cook over medium-low heat for 5 minutes. Add the milk and slowly heat it without bringing to a boil. Cook, stirring occasionally, until the turnips are tender.

Cool the soup briefly, and then purée it in a blender. If needed, add a bit more milk or water. Add freshly ground pepper.

Sort through the greens and wash them. Melt the remaining 2 Tbs. butter in a pan, add turnip greens, and cook over medium heat until they are tender, about 5–10 minutes. Season with salt and pepper. Remove the greens to a cutting board and chop them. Add the greens to the soup and serve, garnished with chopped thyme.

Serves 4–6.

Cheesy Cauliflower Soup

2 large potatoes, scrubbed and diced
1 large cauliflower, cleaned and broken into florets
2 medium carrots, scrubbed and chopped
3 medium garlic cloves, minced
1½ cups chopped onion
1½ teaspoon salt
4 cups water
2 cups grated Cheddar cheese (packed if you want it real cheesy,
    measured loosely if you want soup less cheesy)
¾ to 1 cup soymilk, depending on consistency you like
1 tsp. dried dill
½ tsp. caraway seeds
Black pepper, to taste

Place the potatoes, cauliflower, carrots, garlic, onion, salt, and water in a large pan. Bring to a boil, and then turn down heat and simmer until the vegetables are very tender. Cool for 5 minutes.

Purée part or all* of the soup in a blender or food processor, and return to pan.

Add the rest of the ingredients to the soup. Heat gently and serve with a bit of shredded cheese.

*If you choose to purée all of the soup, you may want to keep out 2 cups of the cauliflower from the original cooking. Steam this separately, and add them to the purée along with the rest of the ingredients.

Serves 6.

Pumpkin Soup

2 pounds of cooking pumpkin, peeled, seeded, and cubed
1 tsp. cumin seeds
1 tsp. coriander seeds
1 Tbs. sesame seeds
1 Tbs. olive or pumpkin-seed oil
1 red onion, chopped
2 garlic cloves, crushed
1 tsp. ground ginger
1 lime, juiced and zested
4 cups vegetable broth
2 tsp. sugar
Fresh cilantro or coconut to garnish

In a dry frying pan, lightly toast the seeds, taking care not to let them burn. Then crush them in a mortar and pestle.

Heat the oil in the pan and fry onion and garlic over medium heat, without browning, until soft. Add the ground spices, ginger, and lime zest, and stir well.

Then add the broth, lime juice, sugar, and pumpkin cubes. Bring to a boil; then simmer until the pumpkin is soft—about twenty minutes.

Cool and then liquidize the soup in batches until smooth. Reheat gently to serve.

Ladle into bowls, and garnish with toasted coconut or cilantro leaves.

Serves 4.

Pumpkin Pecan Soup

Olive oil to coat pan
1 medium yellow onion, chopped
1 large leek, white part only, cleaned and chopped
3 garlic cloves, minced
1 Tbs. fresh ginger, peeled and minced
1 tsp. cinnamon
½ tsp. cardamom
¼ tsp. cloves
3 pounds pumpkin, cooked or canned
2 cups vegetable broth
2 Tbs. soy sauce or tamari
1 tsp. white pepper
1 Tbs. sea salt (if desired)
½ cup pecans

In a large sauce pan, heat the oil. Then at medium heat, sauté the onions until transparent. Add leeks, garlic, ginger, cinnamon, cloves, and cardamom to the mixture, cooking for 2 more minutes.

Whisk pumpkin and vegetable broth into onions, and simmer for about 45 minutes to 1 hour.

About 10 minutes prior to serving, add the soy sauce and white pepper. Top with pecans.

Serves 4–6.

Pumpkin Yogurt Soup

2½ pounds cooking pumpkin, peeled, cleaned, cut into 2-inch
    chunks (or 3 15-oz. cans of pumpkin less □ cup)
4½ cups hot water
2 vegetable boullion cubes
1–2 tsp. sugar
Salt and pepper to taste
1 cup room-temperature Greek style yogurt (or whole milk yogurt)
Cinnamon to taste

Dissolve boullion in hot water. Cook pumpkin in 1½ cups of that vegetable broth for about 15 minutes or until tender. Purée pumpkin and liquid in food processor, and then return to the pot with sugar, salt, and pepper. Add the remaining broth.

Heat for another 5 minutes.

If using canned pumpkin, pour all the vegetable broth into a pan, add the pumpkin, salt, pepper, and sugar. Cook for 20 minutes until hot, adding water to thin it, if necessary.

Serve hot with a dollop of yogurt in the center of each bowl. Sprinkle with cinnamon.

Serves 4.

Pumpkin Harvest Soup

2 pumpkins or butternut squash, peeled, seeded, and cut into
    chunks of about 2 inches
5 shallots, thinly sliced
½ onion, thinly sliced
Stalk of celery
Large carrot
3 garlic cloves
1 cup brown sugar
2 Tbs. ground cinnamon
2 tsp. ground nutmeg
¼ tsp. mace
2 quarts vegetable broth
2 cups whipping cream
½ pound of melted butter
Salt and pepper to taste

Toss the pumpkin with half of the butter and half of the spices. Add half the sugar, and mix it all as best you can. Place the pieces on a cookie sheet, and roast in a 350-degree oven until tender.

In a large stock pot, add the remaining butter and vegetables, cooking until tender, but not brown. Now add the roasted pumpkin and the remaining spices. Gently stir in the cream. Simmer for 20 minutes.

Remove from heat, and place the soup in a blender. Purée the soup gently.

Serves 8.

Carrot Soup

10 medium carrots, peeled or scrubbed and cut into chunks
Milk of your choice
2 Tbs. clarified butter
⅛ tsp. ground ginger
⅛ tsp. cinnamon
⅛ tsp. turmeric
¼ tsp. ground cumin
½ tsp. coriander
Dash of nutmeg
1 small onion, chopped
¼ cup chopped fresh parsley
Basil, as desired
Summer savory, as desired
Salt and pepper to taste
Juice of 1 orange (optional)

Boil carrots in enough water to cover them. When cooked and cooled, place carrots in a blender with the water they were boiled in. Blend, adding milk as needed to get the desired thickness. Return to the cooking pan and set aside.

In a cast-iron skillet (if possible) fry ginger, cinnamon, turmeric, cumin, coriander, and nutmeg in butter. Add onion and fry, stirring frequently, until it is translucent. Add a little water, if necessary, to keep from burning. Add parsley, basil, and savory to taste. Cook for a minute more until the herbs are soft.

Add the spices to the blended carrots, and bring to a boil. Add salt and pepper to taste. Add orange juice just before serving.

Serves 4–6.

Gingered Carrot Soup

2 firm and ripe avocados
3 cups fresh carrot juice
¾ tsp. salt
5 tsp. fresh lime juice
2¼ tsp. peeled and finely grated fresh ginger
Pinch of curry powder

Quarter avocados, pit, and peel. Purée 1 avocado with carrot juice, salt, 4 teaspoons of the lime juice, and 2 teaspoons of the ginger in a blender until very smooth.

Cut the remaining avocado into ¼-inch pieces. Gently toss them with the remaining lime juice, ¼ teaspoon ginger, the curry powder, and a pinch of salt.

Serve the soup garnished with the seasoned avocado.

Serves 2–4.

Black Bean Potato Soup

1½ cups black beans
6 cups water
1 onion, chopped
2 Tbs. olive oil
2 large garlic cloves, minced
4 stalks celery with leaves, chopped
2 large potatoes, diced
2–3 carrots, diced
1 bay leaf
1 tsp. oregano
½ tsp. ground cumin
1½ tsp. salt
⅛ tsp. black pepper

Wash beans and put them in a pan along with the water. Cover loosely, bring to a boil, and simmer for 2½ hours or until the beans are quite tender.

While the beans cook, sauté onion and garlic in the oil until soft. Chop celery (include the leaves), and dice potato and carrot. Add them to the onion, and heat for several minutes, stirring all the while.

Add all the vegetables to the beans, along with the seasonings, in the last hour of their cooking. Bring the soup to a boil and then lower the heat to simmer until the beans and vegetables are done.

Serves 6.

Black Bean Tomato Soup

12 sun-dried tomatoes (not in oil)
1 cup boiling water
1½ cups finely chopped onions
6 garlic cloves, pressed
1–2 Tbs. olive oil
1 heaping tsp. cumin
1 heaping tsp. coriander
12 cups water
3 cups diced or crushed tomatoes with juice
4–6 cups (two or three 16 oz. cans) black beans
¼ cup chopped fresh cilantro
Additional water or tomato juice
Plain nonfat yogurt
Salt and pepper to taste

In a small bowl, cover sun-dried tomatoes with boiling water, and set aside.

In a soup pot, sauté onion and garlic in oil for 5 minutes. Stir frequently, until onions are translucent. Add cumin, coriander, ½ cup water, and juice from tomatoes. Let this simmer while you prepare the tomatoes.

Add chopped/crushed tomatoes, cover, and bring to a boil. Then lower heat, and simmer, covered, for 5 minutes.

Add black beans (drained and rinsed), and continue to simmer. Stir occasionally.

Drain and chop softened sun-dried tomatoes. Add them and continue to cook 5–10 minutes more. Stir in cilantro, and add more liquid as necessary.

Garnish with yogurt and cilantro. Serves 10–12.

Black Bean and Sweet Potato Chili

1 Tbs. olive oil
1 medium onion, chopped
1 medium green or red pepper, chopped
1 cup chopped celery
2 garlic cloves, minced
2 tomatoes, diced
2 15-oz. cans of black beans, drained
1 28-oz. can crushed tomatoes
1–2 Tbs. chili powder
1 Tbs. dried parsley
2–3 tsp. ground cumin
½ tsp. black pepper
½ tsp. salt
2 large sweet potatoes, scrubbed and diced (2–3 cups)

In a large pan, heat the oil. Add the onion, pepper, celery, and garlic, and cook for another 7 minutes, over medium heat, stirring frequently.

Stir in tomatoes and cook 3–4 minutes more. Stir in beans, crushed tomatoes, and seasonings, and cook for about 30 minutes, stirring occasionally.

In a separate pan, place sweet potatoes in enough boiling water to cover. Cook for about 15 minutes until tender, then drain. When the chili has cooked for about 25 minutes, stir sweet potatoes into the pot and enjoy!

Serves 6.

Lentil Rice Stew

1 Tbs. olive oil or clarified butter
1 onion, chopped
4 garlic cloves, minced
1 sweet red pepper, chopped
2 medium potatoes, scrubbed and chopped
1 bay leaf
4 medium carrots, scrubbed and chopped
2 cups green or brown lentils
5 bouillon cubes, mixed with 10 cups of water
Dried thyme and ground cumin to taste
1 cup of cooked basmati rice

Lightly sauté onion, garlic, red pepper, potatoes, bay leaf, and carrots in clarified butter or olive oil.

Sort and wash the lentils.

Fill a soup pot with water, bouillon cubes, sautéed veggies, and rest of ingredients, except the rice. Boil ingredients for 15 minutes, and then simmer for another ½ hour or so.

Add rice and simmer another 15 minutes. Serve the stew in large bowls with bread and butter.

Serves 12.

Lentil Spinach Stew

1 cup dry lentils
1 medium onion, chopped
2 cloves garlic, minced
4 cups vegetable broth
1 14½-oz. can diced tomatoes in juice
1 Tbs. Worcestershire sauce
½ tsp. salt
½ tsp. dried thyme
¼ tsp. crushed fennel seed
¼ tsp. black pepper
1 bay leaf
1 cup chopped carrot
10 oz. chopped frozen spinach, thawed and squeezed dry
1 Tbs. balsamic or red wine vinegar

Clean and rinse lentils. Set aside.

Sauté onion and garlic in small amount of broth until tender, not brown. (Watch that all of the liquid doesn't evaporate or onion will stick to pan, but too much liquid will simmer instead of sauté.) Add tomatoes and stir.

Stir in lentils and broth with spices. Bring to a boil. Cover and simmer 20 minutes.

Add carrots, and spinach. Bring to a boil again. Cover pot and simmer until lentils are tender.

Stir in vinegar and discard bay leaf.

Serves 6–8.

Italian Lentil Soup

2 medium carrots, sliced (about 1 cup)
1 stalk celery, sliced (about ½ cup)
1 small onion, chopped (about 1/3 cup)
1 Tsp. olive oil
5 cups water
½ of a head of cabbage, cored and cut into 1-inch pieces (4 cups)
1 cup dry lentils, rinsed and drained
1 cup tomato purée
1½ tsp. sugar
1½ tsp. salt
½ tsp. dried oregano, crushed
¼ tsp. black pepper

In a large saucepan cook carrots, celery, and onion in hot olive oil for about 5 minutes or until crisp-tender.

Stir in water, cabbage, lentils, tomato purée, sugar, salt, oregano, and pepper. Bring to boil and then reduce heat. Cover and simmer for 45 minutes or until lentils are very soft.

Serves 5.

Miso Soup

1 tsp. sesame oil
1 onion, sliced
Pinch of sea salt
5 cups water
2 cups chopped greens
1 carrot, sliced thin
¼ cup miso

Place soup pot on medium heat and add oil. When the oil is hot, add onions and stir to cook, about 2–5 minutes.

Add salt, water, and remaining vegetables and bring to a boil. Then reduce heat and simmer, covered, for 20–30 minutes or until veggies are just tender. Remove from heat.

Dilute miso with about ¼ cup of the soup broth and then stir the miso into the soup. Don't boil the soup again after adding miso, as the boiling kills beneficial digestive-aiding enzymes and destroys some of its nutritional value.

Cover the pot and allow the soup to steep for about 5 minutes before serving.

Serves 4.

Miso Noodle Soup

8 cups water
2 tsp. minced garlic
2 tsp. minced fresh ginger
¼ pound udon noodles
1 carrot, thinly sliced
1 head of broccoli, cut in flowerettes
8 shiitake mushrooms, sliced
☐ cup diced yellow squash
12 snow peas, trimmed
½ cup mung bean sprouts
☐ cup mellow white miso
¼ cup barley miso
1 tsp. toasted sesame oil
4 scallions, minced

Combine water, garlic, and ginger in a 3-quart saucepan. Cover and place over high heat, bringing to a boil. Lower heat to medium-high and stir in noodles. Cook for about 3 minutes, stirring frequently to prevent them from sticking together or to the pan. Add carrots to the soup and cook for 5 more minutes. Stir in broccoli and mushrooms and cook for 5 more minutes.

When the broccoli turns bright green and is just starting to get tender, add the squash and snow peas. Continue to cook until the noodles and vegetables are just tender, about 2 more minutes.

Stir the bean sprouts into the soup, and remove the pot from the heat. Combine the two types of miso in a small mixing bowl. Mix enough of the soup broth into the miso to make a smooth paste, then stir the miso into the soup.

Spoon the soup into bowls, and top each with minced scallions and a drop or two of sesame oil. Serves 4.

Adzuki Bean Miso Soup

4 cups water
2 vegetable bouillon cubes
3 cups cooked dried adzuki beans (or rinsed and drained canned
    adzuki beans)
2 tsp. olive oil
3 medium carrots, cut diagonally into thin slices
¼ cup white miso
4 scallions, sliced thin

In a 4-quart heavy saucepan bring water to a boil, and add bouillon cubes, stirring until dissolved. Add the beans and simmer, stirring occasionally, for 15 minutes.

In a heavy skillet, heat oil over medium heat until it just begins to smoke. Stir-fry carrots until crisp-tender, about 3 minutes, then stir carrots into the soup.

In a small bowl, mix together miso and ½ cup of hot broth until combined well. Stir into the soup. Stirring occasionally, bring the soup just to a boil. Stir in the scallions and pepper to taste and serve.

Serves 4.

Tofu Mixed Bean Soup

2 cups mixed beans (kidney beans, black-eyed beans, chickpeas,
   soybeans, mung beans, green beans, black beans, whitebeans,
   red beans)
3 Tbs. cooking oil
1 tsp. fennel seeds
1 tsp. mustard seeds
1 lb. tofu cut into small pieces
2 cups chopped onion
1 Tbs. curry powder
1 Tbs. minced garlic
1 Tbs. minced fresh ginger
½ tsp. turmeric
2 cups chopped tomato
4 cups broth or water
Salt and pepper to taste
2 Tbs. fresh cilantro, finely chopped for garnish

In a large bowl with water soak beans overnight. Then drain the water and wash the beans. Cover and set in a warm place to allow sprouting. It takes about 2–3 days, depending on the desired length of sprouts.

In a saucepan, heat oil; fry fennel and mustard seeds until light brown. Add tofu and brown well. Add 3 cups of sprouted beans, and fry for 2 minutes. Add onion, curry powder, garlic, ginger, turmeric, salt, and pepper. Fry until onions have turned slightly brown. Add tomatoes and broth. Season with salt and pepper. Then bring to a boil, and simmer on low heat until the sprouts are tender and the desired consistency of the soup has been achieved.

Garnish with chopped cilantro. You may serve with rice to make a complete meal. Serves 4.

Tofu Chili

1 pound frozen tofu, thawed, squeezed dry, and cut into cubes
¼ cup water
2 Tbs. low-salt tamari sauce
1 tsp. onion powder
½ tsp. cumin
¼ tsp. garlic powder
1 Tbs. olive oil
1 large green pepper, diced
1 large onion, diced
3 garlic cloves, minced
3 15-oz. cans beans (combination pinto / kidney works best)
2 Tbs. chili powder
1½–2 tsp. cumin
1 tsp. salt
1 28-oz. can tomatoes
1 15-oz. can stewed tomatoes
1 6-oz. can tomato paste
Sour cream or unsweetened yogurt
Shredded cheese

Heat oven to 350 degrees F. Place tofu in a large bowl. Combine the next five ingredients, and pour over tofu, squeezing the tofu so that the liquid is absorbed. Spread tofu pieces on a non-stick cooking sheet, and bake 20 minutes, flip them over, and bake 10 minutes on the other side.

While the tofu bakes, heat oil and sauté pepper, onion, and garlic in a large soup pot until tender.

When vegetables are done, add beans, spices, salt, tomatoes, tomato paste, and the baked tofu pieces to the pot. Simmer and add water as needed. Serve topped with a dollop of sour cream or yogurt and some shredded cheese. Serves 4.

Navy Bean Chili

3 Tbs. olive oil
2 cups chopped onion
2 Tbs. minced garlic
1 cup chopped carrot
1 cup chopped celery
1 cup chopped sweet red pepper
4 cups cooked navy beans
2 cups vegetable broth
1 cup chopped tomatoes
2 tsp. ground cumin
4 tsp. chili powder, to taste
½ tsp. dried oregano
¼ cup chopped fresh cilantro
2 Tbs. pure maple syrup
1 can tomato paste; less if desired
Garnish: cheese, sour cream, or plain yogurt

Heat oil and sauté onions and garlic until soft. Add the carrot, celery, and pepper; sauté 5 minutes.

Add beans, vegetable broth, tomatoes, cumin, chili powder, oregano, cilantro, syrup, and tomato paste; bring to a boil.

Lower heat and simmer, covered, for 45 minutes to one hour. Chili should be thick, but if a thinner dish is preferred, add more water.

Serves 6.

Navy Bean Vegetable Soup

2 cups cooked navy beans
4 cups vegetable broth
1 tsp. olive oil
1 cup apple juice
1 onion, thinly sliced
3 garlic cloves, minced
3 stalks celery, chopped
3 carrots, cut into half moons
1 red bell pepper, chopped
1 cup well-rinsed and chopped kale
2 Tbs. chopped fresh parsley
Salt and pepper, as needed

Cook the beans in the broth until they are ready.

In your favorite soup pot, heat oil and juice. Add onions and garlic; cook, stirring frequently, until onions are soft and golden, about 5–10 minutes. Add celery, carrots, and pepper. Cook and stir occasionally for about 2 minutes. Add the beans and broth.

Bring to a boil. Then lower the heat, cover, and simmer for 20 minutes or until the vegetables are soft. Add kale and parsley. Cook 2 more minutes. Season with salt and pepper.

Serves 4–6.

White Bean Soup

4 Tbs. olive oil
2 stalks celery, chopped
1 onion, chopped
3 carrots, chopped
2 garlic cloves, chopped
1 green or sweet red pepper, chopped
3 cups cooked navy beans
6 cups vegetable broth or water
1–2 tsp. salt, if using unsalted broth or water
1 tsp. freshly ground black pepper
2 tomatoes, finely chopped

Heat 2 tablespoons of olive oil in a large pan over medium heat. Add celery, onion, carrot, garlic, and pepper. Cook until the vegetables are softened.

Purée half of the white beans with the vegetable broth and the remaining 2 tablespoons of oil. Season with salt and pepper. Add tomatoes to vegetables and heat through.

Pour 1 cup of the white bean purée into a soup bowl. Spoon a bit of the vegetables into the center of the bowl. Then spoon 2 tablespoons of the remaining white beans over the vegetables. Repeat with each bowl.

Serves 4.

Hearty Vegetable Stew

½ cup dried shiitake mushrooms
2 potatoes, cut into ½-nch pieces
1 large onion, chopped into ½-inch pieces
1 large carrot, chopped
1 turnip, chopped into ¼-inch pieces
1 parsnip, chopped into ¼-inch pieces
5 garlic cloves, minced
¼ cup wild rice, rinsed and drained
¼ cup barley, rinsed and drained
8 cups vegetable broth combined with mushroom soaking water
1 tsp. salt
1 cup mushrooms, sliced
1 package tofu, cut into 1-inch pieces
2 tsp. fresh dill weed or 1 tsp. dried dill
Freshly ground black pepper to taste
Fresh lemon juice
2 Tbs. chopped fresh parsley

Put mushrooms in a bowl and pour in boiling water to cover them. Let them sit for 30–45 minutes. Remove mushrooms from the bowl, saving the water to add to the broth. Remove and discard mushroom stems; slice the mushroom caps.

Add the mushrooms, potatoes, onion, carrot, turnip, parsnip, garlic, rice, barley, and vegetable broth (or water) to a 6-quart pot. Add the salt. Cook on low for about 8 hours until the ingredients are tender.

Stir in fresh mushrooms, tofu, and dill. Season to taste with the pepper and lemon juice. Add additional salt if desired. Garnish with parsley and serve.

Serves 10.

Winter

Acorn Squash Soup

2 Tbs. clarified butter
2 tsp. ground cumin
¾ tsp. ground turmeric
½ tsp. ground cinnamon
1 cup sliced leeks
5 cups peeled acorn squash cubes
7–8 cups water
3 bouillon cubes
1 cup basmati rice
4 cups chopped Napa cabbage

In a large stock pot, melt clarified butter over medium heat. Add cumin, turmeric, and cinnamon; cook and stir for 1 minute. Add leeks; cook for an additional 2 minutes.

Add acorn squash cubes, water, and bouillon cubes. Bring to a boil. Then reduce heat and simmer, covered, for 10 minutes.

Add the basmati rice. Stir and simmer, covered, for about 30–45 minutes, depending on how long it takes for the rice to be fully cooked.

Add cabbage and simmer, covered, for 5–10 minutes more or until the rice and squash are tender.

Season to taste with freshly ground pepper.

Serves 6.

Hubbard Squash Soup

3 Tbs. butter
3 Tbs. extra virgin olive oil
1 large onion, sliced (about 1 cup)
2 tsp. curry powder
5 pound Hubbard, butternut, or acorn squash, peeled and cut into
   2-inch pieces (about 11 cups)
6 garlic cloves, minced
3 cups vegetable broth
1½ cups water
1 tsp. salt
3 cinnamon sticks

In a 4-quart Dutch oven or pot heat the butter and olive oil over medium heat. Add onion and curry. Cook and stir for 5 minutes or until the onion is just tender.

Add Hubbard squash pieces and garlic. Cook, uncovered, for about 10 minutes, stirring occasionally. Add broth, water, salt, and cinnamon sticks. Bring to a boil and then reduce the heat. Simmer, covered, for about 25 to 30 minutes.

Remove from heat, and discard the cinnamon sticks. Using a potato masher, mash the mixture. (Or cool slightly and transfer in batches to a food processor.)

Return to the pot and heat through. Top with the Poached Lady Apples.

Apples: Cut 2 Lady apples or small apples into 6 wedges each. Core and stem. In medium skillet, combine ½ cup water and 2 Tbs. sugar. Bring to a boil, stirring to dissolve sugar. Add apples, cover and cook 5 minutes or until tender. Remove with slotted spoon.

Serves 8–10.

Everything Soup

8 cups water
4 bouillon cubes
2 Tbs. olive oil
1 onion, chopped
4 garlic cloves, minced
3 carrots, scrubbed and chopped
1 green pepper, diced
4 potatoes, scrubbed and chopped
2 cups tightly packed fresh spinach leaves, well rinsed
¼ tsp. ground black pepper
1 tsp. dried basil
1 tsp. dried oregano

In a large soup pot, boil water and add bouillon cubes.

In a medium skillet, heat oil and sauté onion, garlic, carrots, and green pepper until soft.

When the vegetables are done, add them to the soup pot along with potatoes. Cook until potatoes are soft but not mushy.

Add spinach and spices and cook for another few minutes until the spinach softens.

Serves 6.

Candelmas Soup

2–3 tsp. olive oil
2 medium red onions, chopped
4–5 garlic cloves, minced
4 carrots, scrubbed and finely chopped
1 or 2 red peppers, chopped
1 28-oz. can tomatoes with juice
12 cups vegetable broth
4 cups red lentils, rinsed well
1½ tsp. ground cumin
¾ tsp. ground coriander
Salt to taste if the broth is unsalted
Pepper to taste

In your favorite stock pot, heat the oil and add onion, garlic, carrots, and red pepper. Cook until they are soft.

Add the can of tomatoes and break up the tomato pieces a bit. Add the rest of the ingredients, except the salt and pepper. Bring to a boil, and then reduce heat to a simmer. Skim any brown foam that may form. Cover and simmer for about 1½ hours or until lentils and vegetables are tender and have melded together well.

Serves 8–10.

Chunky Butternut Squash Soup

1 cup chopped onion
2 tsp. olive oil
1 tsp. ground sage
¼ tsp. black pepper
4 cups vegetable broth
2 medium butternut squash, peeled, seeded, and cubed
½ cup enriched vanilla soymilk
Shredded cheese for topping (optional)

In your favorite stock pot, sauté onion in olive oil over medium heat, until soft.

Add the sage, pepper, broth, and squash, and bring to a boil. Reduce heat and simmer for 20 minutes or until squash is tender.

Pour half of the mixture into a blender and purée. Return to pot, add milk, and heat, but do not boil or the milk may curdle.

Serve in bowls topped with a sprinkling of shredded cheese, if desired.

Serves 4.

Harvest Carrot Soup

2 Tbs. olive oil
¾ cup diced onion
2 garlic cloves, chopped
1 Tbs. peeled and chopped fresh ginger
3 cups peeled and chopped carrots
4 cups vegetable broth
2 Tbs. rice
1 cup plain yogurt
⅔ Tbs. cornstarch
Salt and pepper to taste

Over a medium high heat cook olive oil in a small stock pot. Once hot, add onion, garlic and ginger. Sauté until onion begins to soften and turn translucent. Add carrots, vegetable broth, and rice, and simmer for 30 minutes.

Using a blender or food processor, purée the soup until smooth. Return the soup to the pot, and heat over a medium flame.

In a small bowl, combine yogurt and cornstarch, and blend until well mixed. Stir this mixture into the soup, being careful not to bring the soup back to a boil.

Season with salt and pepper, and garnish each bowl with a dollop of plain yogurt.

Serves 6.

Creamy Leek Soup

2 Tbs. olive oil
4 large leeks, rinsed and sliced
4 large potatoes (Russets or Yukon Gold), scrubbed and cubed
6 cups water combined with 3 bouillon cubes
1½ tsp. dried thyme
2 Tbs. fresh cilantro or ½ tsp. dried cilantro
1 cup soymilk
Freshly ground black pepper to taste

Heat oil in a large pot and add the leeks, both white and green sections. Cook over medium heat until leeks are soft. Scrub and cut potatoes into ½- to 1-inch chunks. Place potatoes in the pot and add water/bouillon, thyme, and cilantro. Cook for about one hour, until the potatoes are very soft.

With a large wooden spoon, break up the potatoes. Add the soymilk and cook for another 15 minutes; grind in pepper.

Best served with a salad and warm bread.

Serves 4–6.

Broccoli Potato Soup

2 medium red potatoes, chopped
2 cups broth
3 cups broccoli florets
2 cups milk
3 Tbs. flour
2 cups Gouda cheese, shredded
Black pepper to taste
1 cup winter greens (curly endive, chicory, escarole, or spinach)

In a large saucepan combine the potatoes and the broth. Bring to a boil and then reduce the heat. Simmer, covered, for about 8 minutes. Mash the potatoes a bit in the pan. Then add broccoli and the milk and bring to a simmer.

In a medium bowl, toss flour with the cheese. Gradually add it to the soup, stirring the cheese until melted. Season to taste with black pepper.

Divide among shallow serving bowls, and top with greens.

Serves 4.

Potato and Cider Soup

1 large onion, chopped
1 pound tart apples, peeled, cored, and sliced
2 pounds potatoes, peeled and sliced
1¼ cups apple cider
5 cups vegetable broth
1 tsp. dried mixed herbs of choice
1 tsp. ground coriander
⅔ cup plain yogurt
Salt and freshly ground black pepper to taste
Snipped fresh chives or chopped fresh mint for garnish

Combine onions, apples, and potatoes in a saucepan, and add the cider. Bring to a boil and cook briskly for about 10 minutes, stirring from time to time. Add the broth, dried herbs, and coriander. Cover the pan and simmer the soup for about 25 minutes, until all the vegetables are very tender.

Purée the soup in a blender or food processor, or rub through a coarse strainer. Return to the rinsed pan and stir in the yogurt, reserving 1 tablespoon for garnish. Season with salt and pepper, and reheat without boiling.

Serve with a little yogurt swirled into each bowl and sprinkled with fresh chives or mint.

Serves 4–6.

Potato Kale Soup

2 large leeks, rinsed and sliced
5–8 garlic cloves, minced
8 medium Yukon Gold potatoes, scrubbed and diced
4 stalks celery, chopped
2 small/medium zucchini, diced
4 carrots, scrubbed and diced
8 cups vegetable broth
1 large bunch kale, de-stemmed and chopped
About ¼ cup butter

Bring the leeks, garlic, potatoes, celery, zucchini, and carrots to a boil in the broth. Lower heat and cook until almost tender, about 20 minutes.

Add kale and butter. Cook until the kale is tender and bright dark green, about 15 minutes.

Purée half of the soup in blender until smooth and creamy. Combine with the rest of the soup and heat through.

Serves 8.

Potato Carrot Soup

2 medium bulbs of garlic (about 16 cloves)
8 cups vegetable broth
4 medium to large potatoes, peeled and cut into ½-inch cubes
4–5 carrots, scrubbed and sliced
1 tsp. dried thyme
½ cup soymilk
Freshly ground pepper to taste
Grated Cheddar cheese for topping (optional)

Separate garlic bulbs into cloves and peel them. In a large soup pot, combine broth, garlic, potatoes, carrots, and thyme. Bring to a boil. Reduce heat and simmer, covered, for 20–25 minutes or until vegetables are tender. Cool slightly.

In a blender, purée about half of the soup until smooth. (Do try to purée all of the large garlic cloves.) Return puréed soup to soup pot. Stir in soymilk.

Season to taste with freshly ground pepper.

Top with grated cheese, if desired.

Serves 8.

Potato Cauliflower Soup

½ cup butter
1 large onion, chopped
⅓ cup vegetable powder
6 large potatoes, thinly sliced
1 head of cauliflower, chopped
½ tsp. salt
Freshly ground black pepper to taste

In a medium soup pot, sauté onion in melted butter. When translucent, add potatoes and cauliflower. Cook for ten minutes with salt and pepper.

Add enough water to cover potatoes. Add vegetable powder and simmer until vegetables and potatoes are tender.

Let cool a bit and purée part or all of the soup in a blender.

Reheat and serve.

Serves 2–4.

Potato Cheese Soup

2 cups water
3 medium red potatoes, peeled and cubed
3 Tbs. butter
1 small onion, finely chopped
3 Tbs. all-purpose flour
Crushed red pepper flakes to taste
Ground black pepper to taste
3 cups milk
½ tsp. sugar
1 cup shredded Cheddar cheese
Chopped fresh parsley

Bring water to a boil in a large saucepan. Add potatoes and cook until tender. Drain the potatoes, but reserve the liquid.

Set the potatoes aside. Measure the cooking liquid, and keep 1 cup. (Add more water if necessary.) Set aside.

Melt butter in saucepan over medium heat and add onion. Stir frequently until translucent and tender. Add flour to the saucepan. Season with pepper flakes and black pepper to taste. Cook for 3–5 minutes.

Gradually add potatoes, 1 cup of the cooking liquid, milk, and sugar to onion mixture in the saucepan. Stir well. Add the cheese and stir. Simmer and stir over low heat for about 30 minutes.

Serve sprinkled with chopped parsley.

Serves 4.

Sweet Potato Kale Soup

1 Tbs. olive oil

1 large onion

3½ tsp. dried Italian seasoning (a mix of basil, oregano, rosemary and parsley)

6 cups vegetable broth

2 15-ounce cans beans of your choice; may drain or not

1 pound sweet potatoes (3 large), scrubbed and diced

1 large bunch kale, tough stems removed, coarsely chopped

12 medium garlic cloves, minced

Black pepper to taste

Heat oil in a soup pot over medium heat. Add the onion and seasoning; sauté until onion is soft and golden.

Stir in broth, beans, sweet potatoes, and kale; bring just to a boil. Reduce heat and simmer for 10 minutes.

Add garlic to the simmering soup base. Simmer until sweet potatoes and greens are tender, about 15–20 minutes. Season with pepper to taste.

Serves 6.

Immune Booster Soup

1 ounce dried astragalus root, sliced
1 inch fresh ginger, slivered
½ cup basmati rice, uncooked
8 cups vegetable broth
2 Tbs. olive oil or clarified butter
4–5 leeks, rinsed and sliced or 1 large onion, chopped
1 cup scrubbed and sliced carrots
¾ cup sliced shiitake mushrooms
1 sweet red pepper, chopped
8 cloves garlic, minced
¼ cup miso
¼ cup chopped fresh parsley

In a large saucepan, simmer astragalus, ginger, rice, and broth for 1 hour.

In a separate pan, sauté the leeks, carrots, mushrooms, and pepper in olive oil or butter for 5 minutes. Add garlic and sauté for 1 minute. Add the sautéed vegetable mix to the soup pot, cover, and simmer for 30 minutes.

Remove the astragalus. Dilute miso with a small amount of hot broth, and add to the soup along with the parsley.

Serves 8.

Nepali Lentil Soup

2 cups black lentils (yellow or red lentils can also be used)
2 Tbs. cooking oil
1 cup finely chopped onion
1 tsp. turmeric
1 Tbs. minced fresh ginger
¼ tsp. asafetida
6 cups vegetable broth or water
Salt and pepper to taste

For garnish:
2 Tbs. clarified butter
1 Tbs. minced garlic
½ tsp. Himalayan herb jimbu
1 tsp. cumin seeds
Dried red chilies or chili powder to taste

Rinse lentils thoroughly. In a bowl, put lentils and two cups of warm water; let stand overnight in the refrigerator.

Drain water; rinse off soaked lentils. In a large sauce pan, heat two tablespoons of oil. Fry turmeric, minced ginger, asafetida, salt, and pepper for 30 seconds. Add soaked lentils and stir for a few minutes. Add broth and mix well. Bring to a boil, cover the pan, and allow to simmer for 45–60 minutes or until the lentils are cooked tender and a desired consistency has been achieved. Adjust the seasoning with salt and pepper. Remove from the heat.

In a non-stick frying pan, heat a half cup of clarified butter. Fry garnishing ingredients for a minute or so. Do not allow these frying ingredients to turn dark, or it will impart a bitter flavor to the soup. Drizzle over the cooked lentils and stir gently to incorporate the garnish into the soup.

Serves 6.

Turkish Soup

1 cup red lentils
1½ cups chopped onion
2 Tbs. butter, olive oil, or clarified butter
6½ cups vegetable broth (If the broth is salted, don't add salt.)
2 Tbs. butter
2 Tbs. flour
1 cup soymilk
1 small bag of frozen peas

Pick over lentils; wash, drain, and reserve.

Sauté onions in 2 Tbs. of butter, oil, or clarified butter until soft. Add broth and lentils; cover.

Simmer gently for 25–30 minutes, until lentils are soft. If you wish, purée the soup at this time.

Once the lentils are done and soup is either puréed or left whole, melt 2 Tbs. butter in a pan and add flour. Stir for 2 minutes or so, until the flour turns a golden brown. Add ½ cup of the soup to the flour mixture, and then blend it into the soup. Reduce heat after the soup returns to a boil. Add soymilk.

Add peas; warm the soup gently until the peas are thawed.

Serves 6.

Tofu and Barley Sherpa Soup

4 Tbs. butter
1 cup chopped onions
1 lb. tofu, cut into ¼-inch by ½-inch by ½-inch slices
1 Tbs. curry powder
Salt and pepper
4 cups thinly sliced mushrooms
1 tsp. minced garlic
1 tsp. minced fresh ginger
1 tsp. turmeric
1 cup chopped tomatoes
3 Tbs. soy sauce
1 cup barley
¼ lb. spinach, washed and torn into small pieces
3 cups broth or water

In a non-stick sauce pan, heat butter. Add onions and sauté until lightly browned. Season the tofu with curry powder, salt, and pepper and add to the onion mixture; brown well.

Add mushrooms to the tofu mixture and sauté for 5 minutes or so over low heat. Add garlic, ginger, and turmeric; stir for a minute or so. Add tomatoes, soy sauce, and broth.

Increase the heat; bring to a boil and add barley; stir well. Lower the heat and simmer for about an hour or until the barley grains are tender and a desired consistency of the soup has been achieved.

Finally, add spinach to the soup and wilt it for 1 minute.

Serves 4.

Mexistrone Soup

1 Tbs. canola or olive oil
1 medium onion, diced
1 carrot, sliced
1 large garlic clove, finely chopped
1 small zucchini, halved lengthwise and sliced
1 cup corn kernels, fresh or frozen
1 cup black beans, cooked or canned, rinsed and drained
1 cup pinto beans, cooked or canned, rinsed and drained
1 can stewed tomatoes with jalapenos
2 tsp. dried oregano
1 tsp. dried basil
1½ cups tomato juice
½ cup water
Freshly ground black pepper to taste

Heat oil over medium heat. Add onion and carrot and sauté for about 3 minutes. Add garlic and zucchini and cook with stirring for another 2 minutes. Add corn, beans, tomatoes with liquid, oregano, and basil. Pour tomato juice and water into the mixture and bring to a boil.

Turn down heat and simmer for about 5 minutes. Season to taste with pepper. This soup can be made ahead and refrigerated. It is great served with corn chips.

Serves 6.

Pea Stew with Barley

2 Tbs. olive oil or clarified butter
3–4 leeks, rinsed well and sliced thinly
1 cup sliced celery
4 large carrots, scrubbed and diced
4 garlic cloves, minced
6 cups water or vegetable broth
1 cup dried green split peas, rinsed
½ cup pearl barley
2 large yellow or sweet potatoes, peeled and chopped
2 Tbs. dried parsley
1 tsp. dried thyme
2 tsp. dried oregano
½ tsp. black pepper
2 cups chopped spinach
Salt to taste

In a large pan, heat the oil. Add leeks, celery, carrots, and garlic and sauté for about 8 minutes.

Add the broth or water, split peas, barley, potatoes, and the seasonings, except the salt; bring to a simmer. Cook over medium heat for about 1 hour, stirring occasionally, until the split peas are tender.

Stir in the spinach and cook over low heat for 10 minutes more. Add salt to taste.

Serves 6.

Three Bean Treat

¾ cup dry kidney beans
¾ cup dry pinto beans
¾ cup dry navy beans
16 cups water
2 bouillon cubes
1 large onion, cut into quarters
4 large garlic cloves
⅓ cup tomato paste
1 Tbs. reduced-salt tamari sauce
5 large fresh basil leaves, chopped, or 1½ tsp. dried basil
¼ cup chopped fresh cilantro
¼ cup chopped fresh parsley, or 1 tsp. dried parsley
1 tsp. dried thyme
4 celery stalks, chopped
4 carrots, thinly sliced
1 Tbs. olive oil

In a large, covered pot, bring the beans and 8 cups of water to a boil. Reduce the heat, and simmer the beans for 10 minutes. Remove the pot from the heat, and allow the beans to soak in the hot water until they are cool. May be done overnight.

Drain the beans, rinse them well, and return them to the pot. Add 8 cups of water along with onion, garlic, tomato paste, and the tamari sauce. Bring the mix to a boil. Lower the heat, and cook the beans, covered, for 1½ hours.

Remove the onion, garlic, and half the beans, and place in a food processor; purée the items. Return the mix to the pot. Stir in the remaining ingredients, and cook for about 45 minutes over low heat or until the vegetables and beans are tender. Stir occasionally toward the end of the cooking time to keep the soup from sticking. If the soup is too thick, add a little more water. Serves 8–10.

Orange Soup with no Oranges

2 cups yellow split peas
2 yams, peeled and cubed
1 sweet potato, peeled and cubed
6 carrots, scrubbed and chopped
1 large potato, scrubbed and chopped
2 small onions, chopped
1 small jalapeno pepper, seeded (optional)
16 cups of water
1 bunch fresh cilantro, cleaned and chopped
2–3 tsp. coriander
2 tsp. cumin
1 tsp. tumeric
2 tsp. salt
½ tsp. black pepper
1 bag of frozen peas (optional)

Clean split peas and place in a pot with chopped vegetables and water. Cook for an hour until peas and vegetables are done. Add cilantro and spices. Cook another 15 minutes

Take part or all of the soup to the blender and purée. Return it to pan.

Add frozen peas, and cook another 10 minutes.

Serves 16.

Green Pea Soup

2 cups green split peas
1 parsnip
1 rutabaga
2 small yellow onions
1 large baking potato
1 turnip
1 jalapeno pepper (seeded, unless you like it hot)
1 bunch broccoli
1 bunch fresh cilantro
1 bunch fresh parsley
3–4 carrots
1 Tbs. basil
1 Tbs. coriander
Salt and pepper
Dash of fenugreek

Clean split peas and put in a large pot. Peel and dice parsnip, rutabaga, onions, potato, turnip, and jalapeno pepper, and add to the peas with 4 quarts of water. Cook for about an hour.

During that time clean and chop the broccoli, cilantro, parsley, and carrots. Add to the pot and cook another 20 minutes.

Then spice to taste with the basil, coriander, salt, pepper, and fenugreek. Once the taste is to your liking, purée in a blender.

Serves 20.

Split Pea Soup

2 heaping cups of green split peas
1 onion, chopped
6 carrots, scrubbed and chopped
3–4 stalks celery, washed and chopped
1 bay leaf
3 garlic cloves, minced
½ tsp. dried thyme
10–12 cups water
½ tsp. salt
½–1 cup barley or basmati rice

Put all ingredients in your soup kettle. Simmer, covered, for 3–4 hours or until peas are tender and well cooked. (Time will vary, so begin to check soup at 2½ hours.)

Once cooked, purée some or all of the soup before serving.

Serves 10.

Pinto Bean Stew

3 cups dry pinto beans, and enough water to cover for soaking
12 cups water
3 onions, chopped
2 Tbs. olive oil or clarified butter
2 medium zucchini, rinsed and sliced
5 stalks celery, chopped
3 tomatoes, rinsed and chopped
6 large carrots, rinsed and sliced
1¼ cup basmati rice
1 tsp. salt
1 tsp. ground black pepper
2 vegetable bouillon cubes mixed with 4 cups water
2 Tbs. butter
1 tsp. dried thyme
2–3 tsp. ground cumin

Sort and rinse dry beans and soak in water overnight.

Cook pinto beans in 12 cups of water until soft.

Brown onions in oil or clarified butter in a large soup pot. Add cooked beans and all of the other ingredients.

Bring to a boil, reduce heat, and simmer for 40–45 minutes until vegetables are tender and rice is fully cooked. You may need to add more water to prevent sticking.

Serves 12.

In-a-Hurry Black Bean Soup

2 Tbs. olive oil or clarified butter
2 onions, chopped
4 garlic cloves, finely chopped
1 cup chopped green or sweet red pepper
6 carrots, scrubbed and diced
3 stalks celery, diced
2 tsp. cumin
3 15-oz. cans black beans with liquid
6 cups vegetable broth
1 Tbs. lemon juice
¼ cup finely-chopped fresh cilantro
2 cups cooked rice

In a large pan, heat oil or clarified butter; add onion and garlic; sauté for 2 minutes. Add pepper, carrots, and celery, and sauté for about 4 additional minutes. Add cumin, beans, and broth, and cook for 20 minutes, until vegetables are tender.

Add cooked rice, and heat until all is warmed. Add lemon juice and cilantro, and cook for a minute more.

Top with sour cream or grated cheese, if desired.

Serves 6–8.

Pasta Bean Soup

2 cups sliced fresh mushrooms
1 medium onion, chopped
2 cloves garlic, minced
2 14½-oz. cans vegetable broth
½ cup small pasta shells
16 oz. can diced tomatoes, including liquid
15 oz. can chickpeas, rinsed and drained
¼ cup snipped fresh basil
1 Tbs. snipped fresh thyme

Cook mushrooms, onion, and garlic in a small amount of the vegetable broth until tender, not brown.

Add the rest of the broth to the pot. Bring to a boil. Stir in pasta and cook until al dente.

Stir in un-drained tomatoes and chickpeas. Heat through until hot and fragrant.

Stir in fresh herbs just before serving.

Serves 6.

Roasted Root Soup

1 carrot, cut in chunks
1 rutabaga, cut in chunks
4 artichoke hearts, cubed
3 parsnips, cut in chunks
¼ cup water
1 Tbs. fresh rosemary or ½ tsp. dried
1 tsp. sesame oil
2 tsp. tamari
2 tsp. sesame oil
1 cup chopped mushrooms
½ cup chopped onions
1 celery stalk, chopped
3 Tbs. pearled barley
6 cups water

Preheat oven to 400 degrees F.

Cut root vegetables into small chunks and combine in a baking dish with water. Top with rosemary, and drizzle with oil and tamari. Cover with foil, and roast in oven for 35–40 minutes until tender.

Sauté mushrooms, onions, and celery in sesame oil for about 5 minutes. Add barley and water, bring to a boil, and simmer for 1 hour. Then add the roasted root vegetables and any accumulated cooking liquid to the barley base. Simmer 20 minutes and season to taste.

Serves 4.

Vegetarian Chili

½ cup olive oil

1 large onion, chopped into small pieces

2 red bell peppers, cored and chopped small

4 garlic cloves, minced

2 medium zucchini, sliced and quartered

1 pound fresh plum tomatoes, chopped

1 35-oz. can chopped tomatoes

2 Tbs. chili powder

1 Tbs. ground cumin

¼ cup chopped fresh parsley

1 Tbs. dried basil

1 Tbs. dried oregano

1 tsp. fennel seed

2 tsp. ground pepper

1 tsp. salt

1 15-oz. can each of chickpeas, black beans, red kidney beans, rinsed and drained

½ cup chopped fresh dill

2 Tbs. fresh lemon juice

1 cup sour cream

2 cups shredded Cheddar cheese or Monterey Jack cheese

In a large stock pot, heat olive oil over medium heat. Add the onions, peppers, garlic, and sauté until just wilted, about 6 minutes. Add zucchini and sauté another 6 minutes, stirring occasionally.

Turn heat to medium low and add fresh tomatoes, canned tomatoes, chili powder, cumin, parsley, basil, oregano, fennel seed, salt, and pepper. Cook, uncovered, stirring occasionally for 20 minutes. Stir in chickpeas, black beans, kidney beans, dill, and lemon juice, and cook for another 20 minutes, stirring occasionally.

Serve with sour cream, cheese, and chips. Serves 8.

Vegetable Quinoa Soup

¾ cup quinoa
1 Tbs. canola oil
2 onions, finely diced
3 carrots, peeled and diced
3 stalks celery, diced
2 zucchini, finely diced
½ cup corn kernels
1 bell pepper, red if available, finely diced
1 Tbs. minced garlic
2 tsp. salt
1 28-oz. can whole, peeled tomatoes
1 Tbs. ground cumin
2 tsp. ground coriander
12 cups vegetable broth
½ cup finely chopped fresh cilantro
Black pepper to taste

In a large, heavy skillet, cook well-rinsed quinoa, stirring as you cook for about 10 minutes. When the quinoa becomes golden and the moisture is gone, remove from heat and set aside.

Heat oil in a large soup pot. Add onions, carrots, and celery as you sauté (about 12 minutes). Add zucchini, corn, pepper, garlic, and salt. Continue to sauté until vegetables begin to release their juices.

Squeeze tomatoes into the soup, and add the juice from the can. Then stir in cumin and coriander. Add broth, cover, and bring to a boil. Stir in the quinoa, and then simmer, stirring occasionally for about 10 minutes. The quinoa will then become tender.

Stir in the cilantro; add salt/pepper to taste. Serves 12.

Wild Rice Soup

1 quart vegetable broth
½ cup wild rice
2 Tbs. butter or olive oil
1 cup diced white mushrooms
1 medium-sized yellow onion, chopped
1 tsp. minced garlic
⅓ tsp. dry thyme
½ pound diced baking potato
1½ cups soymilk

Add 2 cups of broth to a medium-sized pot, and bring to a boil. Add rice. When the mixture comes to a boil again, simmer until the rice is tender.

Meanwhile, sauté mushrooms in half of the olive oil until golden brown. Then remove the mushrooms from the pan, and set aside. Add the rest of the olive oil to the pan, and sauté onion, garlic, and thyme until the onion is golden. Add potato and the rest of the broth. Simmer until the potato is very soft and cool. Place in a blender and process until smooth.

Return the blended ingredients to the pot, rice, mushrooms, and soymilk and stir well. Simmer for a half hour. Season with salt and pepper to taste.

Serves 4.

Wild Rice Squash Soup

¾ cup wild rice
3 cups broth or water
2 Tbs. olive oil
4–5 leeks, white part only
3 garlic cloves, minced
¾ tsp. dried thyme
4 large carrots, scrubbed and chopped
2 parsnips, peeled and chopped
2 large potatoes, scrubbed and chopped
2 small to medium butternut squash, peeled and diced
8–10 cups of broth or water, depending on consistency you prefer
Salt and pepper to taste
1 pint half and half

Cook wild rice in 3 cups of broth (or water). It will yield 1–1½ cups of cooked rice. Set aside.

Heat oil in soup pot. Add leeks and garlic, and sauté until soft; then add thyme, and cook an additional 2 minutes. Add carrots, parsnips, potatoes, squash, and water. Heat to boiling. Reduce heat and simmer, covered, until vegetables are soft.

Some or all of the soup may be puréed, as you prefer. Add the cooked rice to the soup and reheat.

Just before serving, add half and half and heat gently but do not boil.

Serves 8.

Wild Rice Vegetable Soup

4 quarts vegetable broth
4 large garlic cloves, minced
¼ cup sun-dried tomatoes (not oil-packed), snipped small
4 large carrots, scrubbed and diced
1 cup sliced celery
1 medium turnip, peeled and chopped
1 green or red pepper, chopped
3 leeks, rinsed and thinly sliced
2 cups shredded Napa cabbage or spinach
1 tsp. dried basil
1 tsp. dried thyme
1 cup wild rice
1 cup brown lentils, washed
4 small potatoes or 2 large Yukon Gold, scrubbed and diced
1 cup frozen peas
Freshly ground black pepper to taste

In large soup pot, bring broth to boil. Reduce heat to simmer, and add garlic and tomatoes. Stir and bring the soup back to steady simmer.

Add the next eight ingredients in the order listed, maintaining a steady simmer. After adding seasonings, simmer 25 minutes.

Add rice, lentils, and potatoes, and simmer 35 minutes more. Then add ground pepper and green peas and cook for another 5 minutes.

Serves 8–10.

Vegetable Chowder

1–2 Tbs. canola or olive oil
1 cup chopped onion
3 cloves garlic, minced
4 carrots, diced
3 stalks celery, diced
1 medium green or red pepper, diced or cut into thin strips
2 cups chopped fresh broccoli
1 cup chopped cauliflower
1 tsp. dried thyme
6 cups water
3 cups potatoes, scrubbed and chopped
8 oz. mushrooms, cleaned and chopped (optional)
2 tsp. dried dill
Salt and pepper to taste

White Sauce: (Double butter and flour for a thicker white sauce)
2 Tbs. butter, 2 Tbs. flour, 2 cups soymilk.

Heat oil in a large soup pot. Sauté onion, garlic, carrots, celery, and pepper 5 minutes or until tender. Stir in broccoli, cauliflower, and thyme, and cook 5–10 more minutes. Add mushrooms and cook for another 2 minutes. Remove from heat.

Bring 2 cups of the water to a boil in a separate pan, and cook potatoes until just tender, about 10 minutes. Then add the potatoes and their cooking water, along with the remaining 4 cups of water to the large soup pot. Bring the soup to a simmer, and stir in dill, salt, and pepper to taste.

Melt butter in a saucepan over medium heat, and whisk in flour. Cook for a minute or so, and then slowly whisk in soymilk. Stir this white sauce into the soup, and simmer for 15 more minutes. Stir occasionally. Serves 8–10.

Sweet Onion Soup

¼ cup olive oil or clarified butter
3 Tbs. butter
12 onions, thinly sliced
½ tsp. sugar
¼ cup flour or 2 Tbs. cornstarch
4 cups vegetable broth
4 cups mushroom broth
1 tsp. Dijon mustard
Freshly ground black pepper to taste
French baguette, sliced thickly
2 cups grated Swiss or mozzarella cheese

Melt butter with oil in a large saucepan over very low heat. Add onions, sprinkle with sugar, and cook until onions are a rich golden brown. Stirring occasionally, this may take up to 2 hours.

Sprinkle flour over the onions, stirring until flour is completely dissolved. Meanwhile combine broths and heat to a boil.

Add boiling broth and mustard to the onions, and blend well. Cover partially and simmer 30–40 minutes. Taste and season with pepper; add more broth if necessary.

Ladle soup into bowls, and top with bread and grated cheese.

Serves 6–8.

Winter Squash Soup

4 cups water
8 cups peeled and cubed acorn squash
2 bay leaves
2 tsp. salt
4 Tbs. olive oil
2 garlic cloves
1 Tsp. diced fresh ginger
½ tsp. turmeric
¼ tsp. black pepper
¼ tsp. asafetida
Unsweetened yogurt
Croutons (optional)

Boil water and add squash, bay leaves, and salt. Boil until the squash is tender. Then remove the bay leaves, and blend the water and squash into a creamy consistency.

In a large soup pot, heat oil and all remaining ingredients for about a minute. Stir frequently to prevent burning. When the spices are ready (giving off their scents), add the squash to the pot. Stir until smooth and heated through.

Add a decorative swirl of unsweetened yogurt to each serving of the healthy soup when served. Sprinkle with croutons also, if you wish.

Serves 4.

Spring

Mixed Mushroom Soup

1 oz. dried porcini mushrooms
2 Tbs. olive oil
2 leeks, halved lengthwise, thinly sliced
Coarse salt and ground black pepper
1 garlic clove, minced
1 pound assorted fresh mushrooms: white, crimini, oyster,
   shiitake (stemmed), rinsed and chopped
½ tsp. fennel seeds
2 bay leaves
1 Tbs. tomato paste
1 14.5-oz. can diced tomatoes, drained
4 cups vegetable broth

Soak porcini in 1 cup warm water until softened (20 minutes). Lift porcini from liquid, and coarsely chop them. Strain liquid through a cheesecloth-lined sieve and reserve.

In a large pot, heat oil over medium flame. Add leeks, season with salt and pepper, and cook for 5 minutes or until tender.

Add garlic, porcini, and other chopped mushrooms. Season with salt and pepper. Cook for 7 minutes or until mushrooms just begin to brown. Add fennel seeds, bay leaves, tomato paste, and tomatoes, and cook for 3 minutes. Add porcini liquid and broth.

Reduce heat to low, and simmer for 30 minutes. Discard bay leaves before serving.

Serves 6.

Mushroom Soup with Herbs

3 Tbs. butter or clarified butter
2 medium onions, finely chopped
2 garlic cloves, minced
1 pound (about 6 cups) fresh mushrooms, thinly sliced
2 carrots, diced
2 celery ribs, very thinly sliced
3 Tbs. flour or 1½ Tbs. cornstarch
7 cups vegetable broth
½ tsp. salt
Freshly ground black pepper to taste
¾ cup cream or soymilk
2 Tbs. minced fresh chives
½ tsp. minced fresh thyme or ¼ teaspoon dried thyme

Melt butter in a large stock pot over medium heat. Add onions and garlic, and sauté 10 minutes, or until tender. Stir often.

Raise heat to medium-high. Stir in mushrooms, carrots, and celery, and cook until the mushrooms are tender and juicy, about 10 minutes.

Sprinkle on the flour, and stir to mix. Cook 2 minutes, stirring frequently. Stir in the vegetable broth, salt, and pepper, and bring the soup to a boil, scraping the bottom of the pot with your spoon to remove any flour bits that have stuck.

Cook 30 minutes at a lively simmer, stirring often. Remove about 2–4 cups of the soup from the pot, and purée in a blender or food processor, then return to the pot.

Mix in cream/soymilk, chives, and thyme. Bring to a boil again; then remove from the heat. Serve immediately, or reheat when ready to serve. Serves 8.

Cauliflower Soup

2 tsp. olive oil
1 cup chopped red onion
½ cup chopped celery
4 cauliflower florets (about 1½ pounds)
½ tsp. ground coriander
3 cups vegetable broth
⅓ cup fat-free evaporated milk
¼ tsp. salt
⅛ tsp. freshly ground black pepper

Heat olive oil in a soup pot over medium heat. Add onion and celery, and cook, stirring occasionally, for 6 to 7 minutes. Stir in the cauliflower and coriander, and cook 2 minutes.

Add vegetable broth, and bring to a boil. Reduce the heat to medium-low, cover, and simmer 20 minutes or until tender. Remove from the heat and cool about 5 minutes.

Purée the soup in batches, and then return it to the pot. Stir in milk with salt and pepper. Warm over medium heat until heated through, about 5 minutes.

Serves 4.

Tomato and Lime Soup

3 Tbs. vegetable oil
1 cup chopped onions
4 large garlic cloves, minced
1–2 minced chilies (1 inch long)
1 tsp. ground cumin seeds
½ tsp. dried oregano
3½ cups chopped fresh tomatoes
3 cups vegetable broth
⅓ cup fresh lime juice
Salt to taste
Grated Monterey Jack cheese
Tortilla chips, crumbled
Chopped fresh cilantro

In a medium soup pot, sauté onions and garlic in oil until the onions are translucent. Add chilies, cumin, and oregano, and sauté for a few more minutes. Add chopped tomatoes and sprinkle with a little salt. Cover the pot, and cook gently until the tomatoes begin to release their juices. Stir occasionally.

Add broth and simmer, covered, for about 15 minutes. Add lime juice and salt to taste.

Serve topped with cheese and crumbled tortilla chips. Garnish with cilantro.

Serves 4.

Feta Soup

¼ cup olive oil
1 cup chopped onions
½ cup chopped fresh basil
½ tsp. salt
2 bay leaves
3 garlic cloves, chopped
5–6 ripe, fresh tomatoes, peeled and diced
3 cups vegetable broth
1 cup crumbled feta cheese
2 cups tomato sauce
Black pepper to taste

Heat olive oil in saucepan. Add onions and sauté until they become translucent (approximately 2 minutes). Stir in salt, add bay leaves and garlic, and sauté for 2 more minutes.

Add tomatoes and vegetable broth. Bring to a boil, and then cook over high heat for 20 minutes, stirring often. Remove from heat.

Remove bay leaves, and let the soup cool a bit. Then place soup, in small batches, in a blender or food processor, and blend until smooth.

Pour all the soup mixture back into the saucepan, and add basil, feta cheese, tomato sauce, and black pepper. Simmer for 20 more minutes.

Serves 6.

Curried Chickpea Soup

½ cup cooking oil
1 tsp. cumin seeds
1½ cups diced onion
1 cup diced green pepper
1 cup diced celery
1 Tbs. grated fresh garlic
1 Tbs. grated fresh ginger
1 Tbs. chopped chili pepper
1 Tbs. cumin powder
2 cups diced potatoes
1 tsp. turmeric
2 cups chickpeas, presoaked overnight
1 cup diced tomatoes
2 cups broth or water
Salt and black pepper to taste
½ cup chopped fresh cilantro for garnish

In a large non-stick sauce pan, heat oil and fry cumin seeds for a minute or so. Add diced onions, green pepper, and celery; fry until lightly browned. Add garlic, ginger, chili, and cumin powder for a couple of minutes over low heat. Bring heat to medium-low. Add potatoes and stir-fry for 5 minutes or until potatoes are half cooked. Add turmeric and mix well for a few seconds.

Put soaked chickpeas into the potato mixture, and give it a good stir for 5–7 minutes. Add tomatoes, broth, salt, and pepper. Allow to simmer for 40–60 minutes or until the chickpeas are tender and the desired consistency of the soup has been achieved.

Garnish with cilantro.

Serves 4.

Chili with Quinoa

1 cup quinoa, well rinsed
2 cups water
1 Tbs. canola or olive oil
1 large onion, chopped
1 medium green pepper, diced
1 cup diced celery
2–3 large carrots, scrubbed and diced
2 tomatoes, diced (optional)
2 15-oz. cans kidney, adzuki, or black beans, drained
1 28-oz. can crushed tomatoes
1–2 Tbs. chili powder
1 Tbs. dried parsley
1 Tbs. dried oregano
2 tsp. ground cumin
¼ tsp. black pepper
½ tsp. salt

In a medium pan, combine quinoa with water and cover. Bring to a simmer and cook for 15–20 minutes or until all of the liquid is absorbed. Remove from heat and let stand for about 10 minutes.

In a large pan, heat the oil and add onion, pepper, celery, and carrot. Cook for 7 minutes until tender; stir frequently. Add the fresh tomatoes and cook for another 4 minutes.

Stir in beans, crushed tomatoes, and seasonings, and cook for about 25 minutes, over low heat, stirring occasionally. Add the cooked quinoa, and cook another 5 minutes.

Serves 4–6.

Cream of Broccoli Soup

1 Tbs. olive oil

2–3 leeks, rinsed thoroughly and sliced

2 garlic cloves, minced

2 stalks celery, chopped

2–3 carrots, scrubbed and chopped

4 cups fresh broccoli, cut into florets

2 cups vegetable broth

½ tsp. dried thyme

½ tsp. dried basil

1 cup ricotta cheese

1 cup soymilk

1 tsp. lemon juice

¼ tsp. salt or to taste

½ tsp. black pepper

Heat oil in pan. Sauté leeks and garlic until soft. Add celery and carrot, and cook for an additional 5 minutes.

Add broccoli, broth, thyme, and basil; bring to a boil. Reduce heat, cover, and simmer 10–15 minutes or until broccoli is tender. Remove from heat.

In a blender, combine ricotta cheese and soymilk until smooth. Add to the soup. Stir in lemon juice, salt, and pepper.

Purée some, none, or all of the soup in batches. Return to pan, and heat through, but do not boil. Stir frequently.

Serves 4–6.

Creamy Spinach Soup

8 cups water
3 medium-sized potatoes, diced
1 onion, chopped
1 tsp. salt
4 cups chopped fresh spinach
½ pint sour cream
2½ Tbs. cornstarch
¼ cup water
2 tsp. dill weed
1 tsp. salt or to taste
Freshly ground black pepper to taste

Add potatoes, onion, and salt to water. Bring to a boil, turn heat to low, and simmer until the potatoes are soft.

Add spinach to the potato mixture; cover and cook for about 5 minutes more.

Purée half of the mix in a blender or food processor, and return it to the pot.

In a small bowl, mix sour cream, cornstarch, and water until smooth and without any lumps. Add the sour cream mixture to the soup. Bring to a boil, stirring occasionally, until the soup thickens. Add dill weed, salt, and pepper.

Serves 8.

Corn Chowder

2 Tbs. clarified butter or butter
1 cup chopped onion
¾ to 1 cup chopped celery
1 sweet red pepper, chopped
1–2 bags frozen corn or 4 cups fresh corn
½ tsp. salt
Freshly ground black pepper to taste
¼ tsp. thyme
½ tsp. dried basil
1–2 cups vegetable broth
1 cup soymilk or evaporated milk

Cook onions in butter over medium heat, stirring. After about 5 minutes add celery and continue to cook. After another 5 minutes, add peppers and corn. Stir in seasonings and cover. Reduce heat and cook 5 minutes.

Add broth. Cover and simmer for about 10 minutes. Purée half the soup in a blender and then add to the rest.

About 10 minutes before serving, add milk. Heat gently.

Serves 4.

Corn Chowder with Vegetables

1 Tbs. clarified butter
1 cup sliced onions
2 cups pared, cubed potatoes
¾ cup thinly sliced carrots
1 cup chopped celery
3 vegetable bouillon cubes
¾ tsp. salt
¼ tsp. black pepper
¼ tsp. dried marjoram
½ cup water
2½ cups cream style corn
3½ cups milk

Sauté onions in butter until tender. Add potatoes, carrots, and celery, and sauté for 2 minutes more.

Add remaining ingredients except corn and milk. Cover and simmer over low heat until potatoes are tender, about 15 minutes. If you wish thicker chowder, sprinkle ¼ cup of flour over the sautéed vegetables at this point.

Now add corn and milk and heat thoroughly. You may wish to blend part of the chowder to make it more liquid, or serve it chunky.

Serves 4.

Greek Soup

2–3 medium leeks
1 pound spinach
2 tsp. butter
2 tsp. olive oil
1 small potato, peeled and cubed
3 cups vegetable broth
1 cup coconut milk
¾ cup Greek style yogurt (or 1½ cups regular yogurt strained
    through a cheesecloth)
Chili powder to taste
Zest of one lemon
Salt and pepper

Trim leeks down to the whites. Slice each stalk in half, then cut in ¼-inch half circles. Wash well. Wash the spinach well, and trim the stems.

Heat butter and oil in a large saucepan. Add the leeks and a pinch of salt, and sauté until very soft (about 10 minutes). Stir often, being careful not to burn. Add potato. Then add vegetable broth and simmer until potato is soft. Add spinach.

Bring the mixture to a simmer; add coconut milk. Simmer 10 more minutes. Remove soup from heat, and when slightly cooled, purée in a blender or food processor.

Mix yogurt with chili powder and set aside.

Pour the puréed broth back into the pan, add lemon zest, salt, and pepper to taste. If necessary, thin with water or broth, or to thicken, cook a little longer.

May be served either warm or cold with a dollop of yogurt.

Serves 4–6.

Brown Rice and Broccoli Soup

2 Tbs. olive oil
1 large onion, chopped
4 medium garlic cloves, minced
10 cups vegetable broth
2 cups cooked basmati rice
About 4 cups broccoli florets, cut into bite-size pieces
½ tsp. dried thyme
2 Tbs. chopped fresh basil leaves

Heat oil in large pot. Add onion and sauté over medium heat until golden. Add garlic and cook about 2 minutes. Add broth and bring to a boil.

Stir in cooked rice and heat for about 5 minutes. Add broccoli and cook, uncovered, until broccoli is tender, about 5 minutes. Stir in thyme and basil and cook 1 minute more.

Serve immediately so broccoli doesn't become overcooked.

Serves 8–10.

Spinach Polenta Soup

½ cup plus 4 more tsp. extra-virgin olive oil
3 garlic cloves, minced
6 cups water
½ cup yellow cornmeal
½ cup finely grated Parmesan cheese
3 cups coarsely chopped baby spinach
1 tsp. coarse salt
Freshly ground pepper
Fresh lemon wedges

Heat ¼ cup of the olive oil in a saucepan over medium heat. Add garlic and cook about one minute or until it is fragrant.

Add the water and bring to a boil. Whisking constantly, add cornmeal in a slow, steady stream. Then reduce heat to medium and cook, stirring occasionally, until it has thickened slightly, about 8 minutes.

Add cheese and ¼ cup olive oil. Cook and stir, incorporating the oil, about 1 minute.

Stir in spinach and salt. Cook, stirring, until spinach is bright green and wilted, about 1 minute more.

Divide soup into bowls, and drizzle each serving with oil in a spiral (about 1 tsp. per bowl). Season with black pepper and serve with lemon wedges.

Serves 4.

Spinach and Lentil Soup

2 cups yellow lentils
2 cups broth or water
2 cups whole milk
1 tsp. turmeric
2 bay leaves
Salt and pepper to taste
2 Tbs. cooking oil
1 tsp. fenugreek
2 cups finely diced onion
2 cups chopped tomatoes
1 tsp. cumin powder
1 Tbs. minced garlic
1 Tbs. minced fresh ginger
1 lb. spinach, washed and cut into small pieces
2 Tbs. butter
1 tsp. Himalayan herb jimbu
5 garlic cloves, thinly sliced

Rinse lentils thoroughly. Place them in a bowl with 2 cups of warm water; refrigerate overnight. The next day, drain water; rinse soaked lentils. In a large saucepan, pour broth and milk, and bring to a boil. Add lentils, turmeric, bay leaves, salt, and pepper. Reduce heat to low, cover, and simmer for 20–30 minutes or until the lentils are tender. Reserve in a bowl.

In a heavy non-stick pan, heat oil and fenugreek. Add onions and fry until brown. Add tomatoes, cumin, garlic, and ginger; fry for a few minutes. Add lentils and spinach, and cook on low heat for a few more minutes. Add more water if a more liquid consistency is desired. Adjust seasoning with salt and pepper.

For garnish, fry jimbu and garlic in butter. Serves 6.

Spinach Soup with Basil and Dill

1 pound potatoes, scrubbed and cubed (Russet or Yukon Gold)
2 cups chopped onion
1 heaping Tbs. minced garlic
6 cups vegetable bouillon
1½ tsp. salt
2 10-oz. packages chopped spinach, thawed and squeezed dry
1 heaping tsp. dried dill
1 handful chopped fresh basil leaves
Black pepper to taste

In large soup pot, on medium-high heat, combine potatoes, onion, garlic, bouillon, and salt. Bring to a boil, reduce heat to low, cover pot, and simmer 20 minutes.

Add spinach, dill, and basil, and cook for 5 more minutes. Add pepper to taste.

Serves 6–8.

Vegetable Soup

6 oz. plum tomatoes (2 or 3 medium sized)
2 Tbs. extra virgin olive oil
1 small onion, chopped
1 large Yukon Gold potato, about ½ pound
2 zucchini quartered lengthwise, cut to ¾-inch pieces
1 celery rib, cut into ½-inch pieces
3½ cups water
1½ Tbs. chopped fresh basil
1½ Tbs. chopped fresh parsley
1 tsp. dried oregano, crumbled
1¼ tsp. coarse gray sea salt
¼ tsp. ground black pepper
2 Tbs. finely grated Parmesan cheese

Prepare tomatoes by cutting a shallow X in the bottom of each tomato with a sharp knife and blanching them in boiling water for 20 seconds. Transfer tomatoes to a cutting board and peel. Then seed and chop.

Heat oil in a 4-quart pot over moderately high heat until oil is hot, but not smoking. Add onion and tomatoes, then reduce heat to moderate, and cook, stirring occasionally, until onion is softened, about 4–5 minutes.

Add potato, zucchini, and celery to onion mixture, and cook, stirring occasionally, about 5 minutes. Add water, herbs, sea salt, and pepper, and bring to a boil, uncovered. Reduce the heat and simmer, uncovered, stirring occasionally, until vegetables are very tender, about 30 to 35 minutes. Remove from the heat.

Serve topped with cheese.

Serves 4.

Vegetable Bean Soup

1 28-oz. can whole Italian style tomatoes
2 medium leeks, sliced
1 Tbs. olive oil
8 oz. fresh mushrooms, quartered
1 large yellow or red pepper, coarsely chopped
4 garlic cloves, minced
3 cups water
1 15-oz. can white kidney beans (Cannellini), rinsed and drained
1 tsp. salt
¼ tsp. freshly ground black pepper
4 cups chopped fresh spinach leaves (about 8 ounces)

Coarsely chop tomatoes, reserving liquid from can. In a 4-quart pot cook leeks in oil until tender, stirring often. Add mushrooms, pepper, and garlic. Cook about 5 minutes more. Add water, tomatoes, canning liquid, white beans, salt, and pepper. Stir and then bring to a boil.

Now simmer the soup, uncovered, for about 5 more minutes. Carefully stir in spinach, and serve.

Serves 6.

Summer

Summer Soup

2 cups ripe mango, cut into chunks (about 4 mangos)
1 cup orange juice
½ cup diced pineapple
½ cup diced melon
½ cup diced cucumber, seeds removed
½ cup diced papaya
2 mint leaves, chopped
Juice of ½ lime
Optional: 1 drop hot pepper sauce
Mint leaves for garnish

Combine mango and orange juice in a blender. Purée for a minute, and strain into a large bowl.

Add the pineapple, melon, cucumber, papaya, and mint to the bowl of juice. Season to taste with lime juice (and pepper sauce, if desired). Cover and chill in refrigerator for at least 30 minutes.

Serve in chilled bowls with mint leaves for garnish.

Serves 4.

Fruit Soup

3 cups strawberries, hulled
3 medium nectarines
3 medium plums
2½ cups blueberries
1½ cups fresh orange juice
6 Tbs. sugar
½ tsp. cinnamon
3 cups water
⅔ cup raspberries
1 cup blackberries
1¼ cups plain nonfat yogurt

Cut large strawberries into quarters, small ones in half. Set aside ½ cup in a bowl and place the remainder in a stock pot. Pit the nectarines. Slice 1 nectarine; add to bowl. Cut remaining nectarines into chunks and add to the stock pot. Pit plums, cut into chunks, and add to stock pot. Place ½ cup of the blueberries in the bowl with strawberries; place the remainder in the stock pot. Place ½ cup of raspberries and blackberries in the bowl and half in the stock pot.

Add juice, sugar, cinnamon, and 3 cups of water to the fruit in the stock pot. Bring to a boil over high heat. Reduce heat and simmer until fruit is broken down and mixture is soupy, about 15 minutes.

Remove from heat and pass through a food mill fitted with a small-holed disk into a large bowl (or you can purée fruit in the food processor). While hot, stir in the reserved bowl of fruit. Let stand until cool, then cover and refrigerate until cold.

Serve chilled soup with a dollop of yogurt.

Serves 10.

Avocado Soup

2 cups tomato juice
1½ cups water
1 avocado
1 small clove garlic
2 tomatoes
2 stalks celery
1 green onion
1 carrot
Seasoning to taste
Chopped fresh parsley

Place tomato juice and water in a blender. Add the vegetables in small pieces and liquefy until smooth. Add seasoning. Garnish with chopped parsley and serve.

The completed soup may also be heated over medium heat if desired.

Serves 4.

Chilled Avocado Soup

3 ripe avocados
2 cups buttermilk
⅓ cup walnut halves
⅓ cup diced red onion
1 Tbs. red wine vinegar
⅓ cup fresh dill sprigs
1 tsp. coarse salt
1 cup water
Topping: extra fresh dill and diced avocado pieces

Halve and pit two avocados. With a spoon, scoop out the flesh, and transfer to a blender. Add buttermilk, walnuts, onion, vinegar, dill, salt, and water, and purée until smooth. Cover the blender, and refrigerate until the soup is well chilled (at least 1 hour).

Halve and pit the remaining avocado. Cut it into four sections lengthwise, and then cut crosswise into ½-inch chunks.

Divide soup among 4 bowls or cups, and garnish each with the diced avocado. Chill until ready to serve.

Serves 4.

Cucumber Summer Soup

3 cucumbers, peeled, seeded, and chopped
1 clove garlic, finely chopped
1 bunch scallions, finely sliced
3 cups vegetable broth
3 Tbs. white vinegar
1 tsp. fresh dill weed or ½ tsp. dried dill
¼ tsp. freshly ground black pepper
2 cups sour cream
1 cup plain yogurt
1 small tomato, chopped
1 Tbs. chopped fresh parsley
1 Tbs. chopped fresh cilantro

Combine first 7 ingredients in a blender.

Mix sour cream and yogurt in bowl.

Slowly add the blended mixture to the sour cream and yogurt mixture. Stir or whisk. Top with chopped tomatoes, parsley, and cilantro.

Serves 4.

Cucumber Soup with Radish Confetti

2 pounds cucumbers, peeled, seeded, and halved
⅓ cup chopped yellow onion
1 cup buttermilk
½ cup plain yogurt
Salt and ground black pepper
⅓ cup diced radish
¼ cup finely chopped green onion tops

Finely dice enough cucumber to measure ¼ cup; set aside. Add the remaining cucumber into a blender or food processor with onion, buttermilk, and yogurt. Process until smooth. Season with salt and pepper. Cover and refrigerate until cold, about 30 minutes.

To serve, divide the soup among chilled bowls, and garnish with the reserved cucumber, radish, and green onion. Serve at once.

For other colorful garnishes, try shredded carrots or finely diced tomato. Chopped fresh dill may be substituted for the spring onions.

Serves 4.

Chilly Cucumber Soup

2 medium cucumbers, peeled and seeded
3 medium scallions (white and green parts)
1 avocado, pitted, peeled, and diced
1 cup vegetable broth
6 sprigs fresh dill or ½ tsp. dried dill weed
1 cup soymilk or buttermilk
¼ tsp. anchovy-free Worcestershire
¼ tsp. salt, or to taste
⅛ tsp. freshly ground black pepper
Chopped fresh cilantro for garnish

Place the cucumbers, scallions, avocado, broth, and dill in a blender. Blend until smooth. Add soymilk, Worcestershire sauce, salt, and pepper. Cover and blend until combined.

Chill for about 30 minutes. Garnish with cucumber, avocado, dill, or cilantro.

Serves 4.

Chilled Cantaloupe Soup

2 oranges
4 generous cups diced cantaloupe
Pinch of salt
2 cups unsweetened apple juice
Zest of the oranges
Ground cinnamon

In a blender or food processor, blend orange juice, cantaloupe, and salt. Gradually add apple juice, blending until smooth. Blend in orange zest to taste.

Chill thoroughly and serve cold with a trace of cinnamon.

Honeydew melon can be used instead of cantaloupe.

Serves 4.

Chilly Strawberry Soup

3 cups strawberries, hulled
1 cup cranberry juice blend, not straight cranberry juice
2–4 Tbs. sweetener of your choice
⅛ tsp. ground nutmeg (optional)
½ cup plain yogurt

Place strawberries, cranberry juice, sweetener, and nutmeg in a small saucepan. Bring to a boil over medium heat. Then simmer, uncovered, for about 5 minutes.

Place this mix in a blender. Cover and blend until smooth.

Chill. Then stir in yogurt and enjoy!

Serves 4.

Chilled Radish Buttermilk Soup

½ pound radishes, trimmed and quartered—about 1¼ cups
2 cups cucumber, peeled, seeded, and chopped
2 cups chilled buttermilk
1 tsp. salt
1 tsp. seasoned rice vinegar
½ tsp. sugar
For garnish: thin slices of radish and cucumber

Purée all ingredients in the blender until very smooth. Pour into small bowls, and garnish with slices of radish and cucumber. Serve immediately.

Serves 4.

Mint Pea Soup

2 Tbs. butter
1 medium onion, finely chopped—about ½ cup
1 clove garlic, minced
5 cups of vegetable broth
4 cups peas, fresh or frozen
2 Tbs. snipped fresh mint
1 tsp. sugar
Coarse salt and freshly ground black pepper
Fresh mint leaves

In a large saucepan cook onion in butter over medium heat for about 5 minutes, stirring occasionally until tender. Stir in garlic and cook 1 minute more. Add vegetable broth and peas. Bring to a boil and then reduce heat.

Simmer, uncovered, for about 12 minutes or until peas are very tender. Add snipped mint and sugar.

Cool slightly. Pour half the soup into a blender and blend until smooth. Follow with the rest of the soup, and blend until smooth. Season with salt and pepper.

Cover and refrigerate until well chilled. Ladle soup into chilled bowls and garnish with fresh mint leaves.

Serves 6–8.

Simple Spinach Soup

10 oz. fresh spinach, washed and chopped
½ large onion, chopped
1 clove garlic
1 cup chopped broccoli
2 stalks celery, chopped
½ cup chopped carrot
3–4 cups water

Put all ingredients together into a saucepan and bring to a boil. Simmer until all the vegetables are tender. Cool.

Place the vegetables and water into a blender and liquefy. Add salt and pepper to taste.

Serve chilled.

Serves 4.

Gazpacho

2 cups cubed day-old bread
2 garlic cloves
Salt and pepper
2 pounds ripe tomatoes, seeded
1 piece cucumber, about 4 inches long, peeled and seeded
1 slice green bell pepper, about 1 inch thick
2 tsp. red-wine vinegar
1 tsp. sherry vinegar
½ cup extra-virgin olive oil, plus more for drizzling
1 cup cold water, plus more for soaking
½ cup extra-virgin olive oil
1 cup cubed bread
Coarse salt and freshly ground pepper

Make gazpacho: Cover bread with cold water, and let soak for 15 minutes. Cover garlic with water in a small saucepan and bring to a boil. Cook for 3 minutes and then drain.

Transfer garlic to a blender. Squeeze excess liquid from the bread, and transfer bread to a blender. Add 2 tsp. salt, tomatoes, cucumber, bell pepper, and vinegars. Purée until smooth. With blender running, pour in oil in a slow, steady stream, blending well. Blend in cold water. Season with salt and pepper. Refrigerate the gazpacho until chilled, at least 3 hours.

Make croutons: Heat oil in a medium skillet over medium heat until hot but not smoking. Add bread and fry, tossing constantly, until gold and crisp, about 7 minutes. Transfer bread to plate lined with paper towels. Season with salt and pepper.

Divide gazpacho among 6 chilled bowls. Drizzle with oil and top with croutons. Serves 6.

Celery Apple Gazpacho

3 cups chopped celery
1 Granny Smith apple, peeled, cored, and sliced
1½ cups cold water
1 Tbs. fresh lemon juice
1 tsp. salt
1 3-inch piece of baguette, crust discarded
¼ cup chopped blanched almonds
2 Tbs. extra virgin olive oil
Garnish: thin celery matchstick curls

Purée celery, apple, water, lemon juice, and salt in a blender until smooth. Chill the mixture in the blender, covered, for one hour.

Reblend, then strain the liquid through a fine-mesh sieve.

Soak the bread in the strained soup for 3 minutes. Rinse the blender, and pulse the almonds until they are finely ground. Add the soup with the bread and blend. Then, with motor running, add oil in a slow stream, blending until emulsified.

Garnish with a strip of curled celery and serve immediately.

Serves 4.

White Gazpacho

3 cups cubed day-old bread
5 garlic cloves
2 cups blanched whole almonds (10 ounces)
2½ tsp. sherry vinegar
Coarse salt and freshly ground black pepper
½ cup extra-virgin olive oil, plus more for drizzling
2½ cups cold water, plus more for soaking
6 seedless grapes, red or green, thinly sliced crosswise

Cover bread with cold water, and let soak for 15 minutes. Cover garlic with water in a small saucepan and bring to a boil. Cook for 3 minutes and then drain.

Pulse blanched almonds in a food processor until finely ground. Squeeze excess liquid from the bread and transfer bread to the food processor. Add cooked garlic, vinegar, and 1½ tsp. salt. Purée until smooth. With machine running, pour in oil in a slow, steady stream, alternating with ¼ cup cold water, blending until emulsified. Blend in remaining 2¼ cups cold water.

Strain through a fine sieve until smooth, discarding solids. Season with salt. Refrigerate gazpacho until chilled, at least 1 hour. Season with salt and pepper.

Divide gazpacho among 6 chilled bowls or glasses. Drizzle with oil and top with grapes.

Serves 6.

Zucchini Cucumber Soup

1 pound chopped zucchini
2 cups chopped cucumber, seeds removed
⅓ cup chopped sweet onion
¼ cup white wine vinegar
¼ cup water
1 tsp. chopped fresh, hot green chili peppers
1☐ tsp. salt
1 tsp. ground coriander
½ cup crème fraiche or sour cream (4 oz.)

Purée zucchini, cucumber, onion, vinegar, water, chiles, 1 tsp. salt, and half the coriander in a blender until very smooth.

Whisk the remaining salt and coriander into the crème fraiche or sour cream.

Serve the soup topped with a dollop of the cream.

Serves 4.

Curried Zucchini Soup

3 Tbs. vegetable oil
2 large onions, diced
2 garlic cloves, minced
1 tsp. minced fresh ginger
1 tsp. turmeric
1 tsp. ground cumin
1 tsp. ground coriander
5 cups vegetable broth
5 medium zucchini, quartered lengthwise and finely diced
½ tsp. salt
Plain yogurt, for garnish

Heat oil in a large stock pot over medium heat. Add the onions, garlic, and ginger, and sauté 10 minutes, stirring often. Sprinkle on turmeric, cumin, and coriander, and cook 2 minutes.

Pour in broth and bring to a boil. Add zucchini and salt, and cook, partially covered, 30 minutes or until the zucchini becomes very tender. Remove the cover, and let the soup cool 10 minutes.

Purée half the soup in a blender or food processor; then return it to the pot. Reheat until hot; then serve in bowls with a generous spoonful of yogurt on each serving.

Serves 6.

Cold Indian Lentil Soup

1 cup red lentils
1-inch piece kombu sea vegetable
8 cups water
1 large onion, chopped
4 large garlic cloves, minced
1 large carrot, chopped
½ tsp. ground turmeric
½ tsp. cumin seed
1 tsp. finely grated fresh ginger
1 tsp. salt
1 cup loosely packed chopped fresh cilantro
1–2 Tbs. fresh lemon juice
Freshly ground black pepper to taste
2 Tbs. minced scallions

Add lentils and kombu to water in a large pot. Bring to a boil for 10 minutes, skimming the foam off the surface.

Add onion, garlic, carrot, turmeric, cumin, and ginger to the pot. Cover and simmer over low heat for about 45 minutes, until the beans and vegetables are tender. Add 1 tsp. salt. Remove from the heat and cool.

Add cilantro and blend the soup in batches, leaving just a bit of texture.

Add lemon juice, pepper, and more salt to taste.

Chill and readjust seasonings if necessary. Garnish with the scallions.

Serves 4.

Index

almonds, 104, 105
apple cider, 4, 45
apple juice, 34, 98
apples
    Granny Smith, 2, 4, 104
    tart, 45
artichoke hearts, 64
asafetida, 52, 72
astragalus root, 51
avocados, 21, 93, 94, 97
beans, 50
    adzuki, 12, 30, 79
    black, 12, 22, 23, 24, 31, 55, 62,
        65, 79
    black-eyed, 31
    Cannellini, 6, 90
    chickpeas, 7, 8, 31, 63, 65, 78
    green, 31
    kidney, 6, 12, 31, 32, 57, 79, 90
    mung, 31
    navy, 33, 34, 35, 57
    pinto, 32, 55, 57, 61
    red, 31
    red kidney, 65
    soybeans, 31
    white, 31
blackberries, 92
blueberries, 92
broccoli, 11, 29, 44, 59, 70, 80, 85,
    102
broth, 9, 46, 87
    mushroom, 71
    vegetable, 2, 3, 4, 5, 7, 8, 13, 16,
        17, 19, 26, 31, 33, 34, 35, 36, 38,
        40, 41, 42, 44, 45, 47, 50, 51, 52,
        53, 54, 56, 62, 63, 66, 67, 68, 69,
        71, 73, 74, 75, 76, 77, 78, 80, 82,
        84, 85, 95, 97, 101, 107
buttermilk, 94, 96, 97, 100
cabbage, 27
    Napa, 37, 69
cantaloupe, 98
carrots, 4, 5, 9, 11, 12, 15, 19, 20,21,
    22, 25, 26, 27, 28, 29, 30, 33, 34,
    35, 36, 39, 40, 42, 46, 47, 51, 55,
    56, 57, 58, 59, 60, 61, 62, 64, 66,
    68, 69, 70, 74, 79, 80, 83, 93, 102,
    108
cauliflower, 15, 48, 70, 75
celery, 2, 4, 7, 8, 12, 19, 22, 24, 27,
    33, 34, 35, 46, 56, 57, 60, 61, 62,
    64, 66, 69, 70, 74, 75, 78, 79, 80,

82, 83, 89, 93, 102, 104
cheese
    Cheddar, 15, 49
    feta, 77
    Gouda, 44
    Parmesan, 86
    ricotta, 80
cilantro
    dried, 1, 43
    fresh, 3, 8, 11, 23, 33, 43, 57, 58,
        59, 62, 66, 108
coconut milk, 3, 84
corn, 55, 66, 82
    cream style, 83
cranberry juice blend, 99
cream, 2, 74
    sour, 4, 81, 95
    whipping, 4, 19
cucumbers, 91, 95, 96, 97, 100, 103,
    106
dates, 8
garbanzo. See beans, chickpeas
ginger
    fresh, 1, 3, 5, 17, 21, 29, 31, 42, 51,
        52, 54, 72, 78, 87, 107, 108
    ground, 8, 16, 20
greens, 28
    turnip, 14
half and half, 2, 13, 68
jimbu, 52, 87
kale, 34, 46, 50
kombu, 108
leeks, 4, 6, 14, 17, 37, 43, 46, 51, 56,
    68, 69, 73, 80, 84, 90
lemon, 1, 8, 36, 62, 65, 84, 104, 108
lentils, 26, 27
    black, 52
    brown, 10, 25, 69
    green, 25
    red, 10, 40, 52, 53, 108
    yellow, 8, 52, 87
lime, 3, 16, 21, 76, 91
mango, 91
melon, 91
milk, 14, 20, 44, 49, 83, 87
    evaporated, 82
    fat-free evaporated, 75
mint, 101
mung bean sprouts, 29
mushrooms, 6, 54, 63, 64, 70, 73, 74,
    90
    crimini, 73

oyster, 73
porcini, 73
shiitake, 29, 36, 51, 73
white, 36, 67, 73
nectarines, 92
noodles
    orzo, 8
    pasta shells, 63
    udon, 29
    vermicelli, 8
oats, 1
oranges, 20, 91, 92, 98
papaya, 91
parsley 11, 20, 34, 57, 59, 65, 89
parsnips, 11, 36, 59, 64, 68
peanut butter, 5
peas
    fresh, 101
    frozen, 53, 58, 69, 101
    green split, 11, 56, 59, 60
    snow, 29
    yellow split, 58
peppers
    green, 7, 12, 24, 32, 35, 39, 62, 66,
       69, 70, 78, 79, 103
    hot green chili, 106
    jalapeno, 58, 59
    red, 6, 24, 25, 33, 34, 35, 40, 49,
       51, 62, 65, 66, 69, 70, 82, 90
    yellow, 6, 90
pineapple, 91
plums, 92
potatoes, 9, 15, 22, 25, 36, 39, 45, 47,
    48, 58, 68, 69, 70, 78, 81, 83, 84
    baking, 11, 59, 67
    red, 44, 49
    red-skinned, 10
    Russet, 43, 88
    sweet, 5, 7, 13, 24, 50, 56, 58
    yellow, 56
    Yukon Gold, 43, 46, 69, 88, 89
pumpkin, 16, 17, 18, 19
radishes, 100
raspberries, 92
rutabagas, 11, 59, 64
shallots, 2, 19
soymilk, 9, 15, 43, 47, 53, 67, 74, 80,
    82, 97
    enriched vanilla, 41
spinach, 6, 26, 39, 54, 56, 69, 81, 84,
    86, 87, 88, 90, 102
squash
    acorn, 37, 38, 72
    butternut, 1, 2, 3, 4, 19, 38, 41, 68

Hubbard, 38
yellow, 29
strawberries, 92, 99
tofu, 31, 32, 36, 54
tomato juice, 5, 23, 55, 93
tomatoes, 7, 8, 10, 12, 24, 31, 32, 33,
    35, 40, 54, 61, 63, 65, 66, 73, 76,
    77, 78, 79, 87, 93, 103
    crushed, 12, 23, 24, 79
    diced, 26
    Italian style, 6, 90
    plum, 65, 89
    stewed, 32, 55
    sun-dried, 23, 69
turnips, 11, 14, 36, 59, 69
walnuts, 94
yams, 11, 58
yogurt
    Greek style, 84
    plain, 45, 84, 95, 96, 99
zucchini, 46, 55, 61, 65, 66, 89, 106,
    107

Yes International Publishers

Justin O'Brien, Ph.D. (Swami Jaidev Bharati)
Walking with a Himalayan Master: An American's Odyssey
The Wellness Tree: Dynamic Six-Steps for Creating Wellness
Running and Breathing
A Meeting of Mystic Paths: Christianity and Yoga
Mirrors for Men
Superconscious Meditation

Linda Johnsen
The Living Goddess: Tradition of the Mother of the Universe
Daughters of the Goddess: The Women Saints of India
A Thousand Suns: Designing Your Future with Vedic Astrology
Kirtan: Chanting as a Spiritual Path

Theresa King
The Spiral Path: Explorations into Women's Spirituality
The Divine Mosaic: Women's Images of the Sacred Other

Swami Veda Bharati
The Light of Ten Thousand Suns
Subtler than the Subtle: Upanishad of the White Horse

Prem Prakash
Three Paths of Devotion
Yoga American Style
Universal Yoga: The Bhagavad Gita for Modern Times

Phil Nuernberger, Ph.D.
Strong and Fearless: The Quest for Personal Power
The Warrior Sage: Life as Spirit

Other Authors
Opening to Dying and Grieving by Ron Valle and Mary Mohs
Circle of Mysteries: Women's Rosary Book by Christin Lore Weber
Pigs Eat Wolves by Charles Bates
The Laughing Swami: Teachings of Swami Hariharananda
The Yogi: Portraits of Swami Vishnudevananda by Gopala Krishna
Soulfire: Love Poems by Rev. Alla Renee Bozarth
Streams from the Sacred River by Mary Erickson and Betty Kling
Mirrors for Women by Cheryl Wall